TRAVELLING THE DEMPSTER
by John Neville

DEAR READER

Writing this small volume has been a memorable experience for me. I have learnt much about the history, flora and fauna of the Yukon and Northwest Territories. By reading this book you will have shared my thoughts, my limited knowledge and my experience along the Dempster Highway. Thank you in advance for making time to travel with me.

Sincerely,

John Neville

DEDICATION

To: Deborah and John,

Fiona, Jamie and Sophia.

Wherever we go, you travel with us in our hearts.

TRAVELLING THE DEMPSTER
by John Neville

TRAFFORD
PUBLISHING

Note for Librarians: A cataloguing record for this book is available from Library and Archives Canada at www.collectionscanada.ca/amicus/index-e.html

ISBN 1-4120-5830-9

TRAFFORD

Offices in Canada, USA, Ireland and UK
This book was published *on-demand* in cooperation with Trafford Publishing. On-demand publishing is a unique process and service of making a book available for retail sale to the public taking advantage of on-demand manufacturing and Internet marketing. On-demand publishing includes promotions, retail sales, manufacturing, order fulfilment, accounting and collecting royalties on behalf of the author.

Book sales for North America and international:
Trafford Publishing, 6E–2333 Government St.,
Victoria, BC v8t 4p4 CANADA
phone 250 383 6864 (toll-free 1 888 232 4444)
fax 250 383 6804; email to orders@trafford.com
Book sales in Europe:
Trafford Publishing (uk) Ltd., Enterprise House, Wistaston Road Business Centre, Wistaston Road, Crewe, Cheshire cw2 7rp UNITED KINGDOM
phone 01270 251 396 (local rate 0845 230 9601)
facsimile 01270 254 983; orders.uk@trafford.com
Order online at:
trafford.com/05-0730

10 9 8 7 6 5 4

ACKNOWLEDGEMENTS

My sincere thanks to:

Norman Barichello for cover photo.

Katarina Boljkovac for her painstaking research.

Bill Hill for allowing me to quote from his web page and many other anecdotes.

Mary Ashworth for her helpful suggestions and meticulous proofreading.

Heather Neville who not only shared the adventure but tolerated the writing of this story. In addition she read, made suggestions and typed the manuscript.

Finally, I take full responsibility for any errors or omissions in this book.

— JEN

CONTENTS

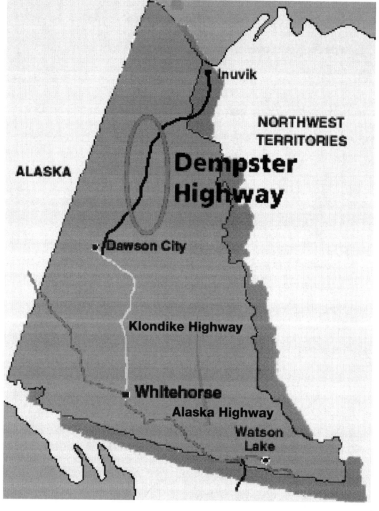

The Dempster Highway - Yukon and Northwest Territories of Canada

INTRODUCTION

Many books and articles have wetted my appetite for an adventure along the Dempster Highway. One such item appeared on April 3rd, 2004, in the Victoria Times Colonist: Lyn Hancock wrote:

"I was awed by its friendly people. Those qualities haven't changed,and its still a long and lonely drive, which is the reason why I'll be back !"

At the end of The Forgotten Trail, Larry Pynn wrote:

"Like the prospectors who travelled this route a century earlier I have felt my fair share of hope and hardship, desire and disappointment. And like so many thousands I leave the Klondike rich not in gold but in experience, memories and personal insight. Moreover I have gained an enduring respect for the people who call the north their home." (34)

As we passed kilometer zero, better known as Mile Zero, on the Alaska Highway I reflected on our objective. I was hoping to record all the common birds and perhaps some of the rare ones for a CD called Bird Songs of the Arctic-Along the Dempster Highway. We were travellers along a good northern highway. Those who journeyed to Dawson 100 years ago had five much harder choices: The Dyea-Chilkoot Pass, Skagway White Pass, the Yukon River when the ice was out, the Stikine River route (the choice of Kate Ryan) (6) or the route starting north from Edmonton via the Athabaska , Slave and Mackenzie Rivers. In 1996, Ian and Sally Wilson tried the Stikine route but found the going too tough!

Gold Rush (42) described the shorter Chilkoot Pass route and their journey floating down the Yukon River. At the end of July, 1900, the White Pass and Yukon Railway created an easy and efficient journey from Skagway to Whitehorse. It was not until 1942 that our route of choice came into being. The Alaska Highway was built in 9 months because of the fear of Japanese invasion during the second World War.

As we followed the Yellow Brick Road to the Klondike a tantalizing question would soon be answered. Are Dawson's streets paved with gold? Many who came this way more than 100 years ago certainly thought so. Like Dorothy we had a sense of wonder as we came closer. Our Toto is a German Shepherd called Falco who is truly the most affectionate dog I have ever had the pleasure to own. If I am awake in the night he will leave his bed and come over to empathize.

Last evening, the 7th of May, we stopped at the edge of Charlie Lake. Thousands of waterfowl were rafting together by species on their journey north. The distinctive calls of the Long-tailed Duck, harsher notes of Bonaparte's Gull, wheeling Franklin's Gull, Goldeneye, Lesser Yellowlegs and many more could be heard. This morning I was able to assemble my recording equipment for the first time on this trip. It took about ten minutes to find all of the necessary items which were stored in four places in the Bird Mobile, the name of our motorhome. Usually I can be out and ready to record in a couple of minutes. Unfortunately, my two new rechargeable batteries would not work which was quite a worry. They seemed okay before we left and I thought the charging process had worked. A phone call to Commercial Electronics in Vancouver helped a little. They assured me that they would take them back if I could not get them to work. The problem is that I need to stay out recording for several hours when the conditions are good. Being away from mains electricity has been solved by having a gadget called an Inverter. Power from the Bird Mobile battery is boosted up to 110 volts. This allows me to plug in my MiniDisc recorder to recharge its batteries.

After a short walk and the chance to record a Robin in full song, we were on the road again. The weather quickly changed into a winter storm! Driving became a challenge and we slowed down as ice and snow piled up on the vehicle. When we stopped at a gas station the attendant admired the 10 centimeter protrusions of ice from our hubcaps! Several cars had slid into the ditch on steep sections. One speeding silver-gray import with youngsters aboard passed at high speed. Shortly afterwards a car ahead of us did a U-turn in pursuit of the silver-gray car. We soon passed both cars parked on the side of the road, one having his flashing lights on! The warning may not have been enough because the same youngsters passed us again at Fort Nelson defying the conditions and doing at least 40 kilometers an hour faster than us. Despite the winter conditions many places along the route brought back memories: the Alpine tundra on Pink Mountain, May's Kitchen which was closed today, and the remote Liard Highway.

The last time Heather drove the Alaska Highway from Dawson Creek to Whitehorse she reflected it was a gravel road. Now most of the way is good pavement. We only experienced one short delay where the surface had been washed out. The winter conditions were a complete contrast to the sunny afternoon we spent with Fiona, Jamie and our granddaughter Sophie just yesterday. Also travelling in our direction were small flocks of White-crowned Sparrows along the roadside, a Sandhill Crane towing long legs, chevrons of geese, just dots in the sky and more regular formations of swans. The raptors were more difficult to recognise in a moving vehicle. Most of them became "an Accipiter" with sharp wings, or a " Buteo" with broad wings. A Golden Eagle dove steeply into a marsh as we passed through the Muskwa Kecheka Management Area. Heather spotted the white rumps of many elk in amongst the trees as evening came on. Our goal had been to reach the Liard Hotsprings but we settled for a quiet spot next to the Toad River. We had turned up this same sideroad two years ago to have one of my most successful days recording ever. Four birds allowed me to capture their songs for the first time; a Gray-cheeked Thrush, Palm Warbler, Blackpoll Warbler and an American Tree Sparrow. These four birds are about to appear in my new CD, Bird Songs-Western Boreal Forest (30).

Another source of interest for our journey north is the Milepost (20). This annual publication is a travel guide of northern highways. For example, we crossed the Sikanni Chief River at kilometer 256. The book explained that several years ago staff from the Tyrell Museum excavated the largest Ichthyosaur ever found from this river bank. It was a marine reptile 23 meters long. That makes it nearly four times longer than the Bird Mobile!

The distances became a blur as we drove for three more days along the Alaska Highway. Muncho Lake Provincial Park was beautiful and we would have liked to stay and explore it further. A female caribou was trotting along the highway and allowed us to catch up. Her brown and gray coat were trimmed with a white bib and socks. She seemed proud to pose for Heather's photograph.

The Liard Hot Springs lived up to their reputation. The water was beautifully warm and relaxing. We soaked it up for an hour or more. A family had journeyed up from Fort Nelson to bath for Mothers' Day. The water ran from the hottest and deepest pool into the lower area that I favoured. It was comfortably warm and the wooden steps made an appropriate bench. The spruce trees surrounding the springs were still tinged with snow and Devil's

Club grew in the undergrowth. The board walk to the springs crossed a rich wetland. Men were repairing the damage in one spot where yesterday's storm had felled a tree. A Canada Goose sat on her nest only a couple of meters from the path. As we reached the carpark a Fox Sparrow serenaded our departure.

A convenient pull-off allowed us to stop and photograph Teslin Lake and the Saint Elias Mountains. After crossing the Teslin Bridge, we decided not to delay for the old American truck graveyard. Just off to one side on the Canol Road many vehicles used to build the Alaska highway were left to rust in 1942. Larry Pynn described them as:

"olive colored trucks, battered, bruised and half gutted shells stripped of their dignity but laid out in neat rows like crosses in a military cemetery." (34)

After our third full day's drive we turned onto the Klondike Highway with 500 kilometers to go before Dawson City. Above an old burn a large bear with a hump was foraging. It was our first Grizzly Bear in the Yukon and we added him to our growing list of wildlife. We crossed the Yukon River at Carmack noting how much wider it had become since receiving the water from the Teslin River. The road led through the boreal forest with occasional glimpses of the Yukon, Stewart and other smaller rivers. We were closing in on our first objective. The Milepost (20) chart had said 1,912 kilometers from Dawson Creek to Dawson City. Stage one was complete.

CHAPTER 1

DAWSON CITY

*Including: Klondike Kate's restaurant, Start of the Goldrush,
Sam Steele & the Mounties, Joe Boyle,
and the Curator of the Jack London Museum*

The road followed the Klondike River into Dawson with huge piles of gravel between the river and the road. One housing development was appropriately called the Dredge Pond Subdivision. The community itself was mainly large wooden buildings. The size of the structures, like the old Northwest Mounted Police station, reflected a time when Dawson was a boom town. There were only 400 souls living in Dawson in the 1970's but now the population has rebounded to 2,000 and growing. The dyke still protects the community from flooding. SS Keno, the old paddlewheeler, was still tied up at the dock. A patch of mud between Front Street and the dyke would soon be green grass and the site of summer activities according to the Klondike Sun. The streets were not paved with gold but reasonably graded gravel. There were well maintained boardwalks all around the downtown, with better provisions for pedestrians than many communities further south. After topping up with gas and water at the Shell Station (which doubled as the Sears outlet) we picked up a few items at the hardware store. It was then time for lunch at Klondike Kate's on the corner of Third and

King Street. Katherine Rockwell was not really associated with the building but it did date back to 1905. The food was excellent and we had already discovered, the people were very friendly and ready to talk. As I sat back talking to a friendly miner, I had flashbacks to Ian and Sally Wilson's visit (42) and Pierre Burton's Drifting Home (11) in 1972. Then my mind went further back to 1896.

The story began with a Nova Scotian, Robert Henderson (Henderson's Corner is named after his son, Grant). He prospected unsuccessfully around the world for 23 years before arriving in the Yukon 1892. After a minor success Henderson returned to the mouth of the Klondike River where he met George Washington Carmack, Taggish Charly and Scookum Jim. They were drying salmon, cutting logs and doing a little prospecting. Henderson told Carmack of possibilities in nearby creeks but his Taggish Indian friends were not welcome. This may have been the worst mistake Henderson made in his life! Carmack was nicknamed Siwash George because of his admiration for the Taggish people, including his wife Kate. When he dreamed about salmon with nuggets of gold for scales and 20 dollar coins for eyes his interpretation was that he should go fishing. Carmack and his Taggish friends left Henderson to work Gold Bottom Creek, while they prospected Rabbit Creek. The friends lifted a pan containing 7.1 grams of gold worth about $4, by far the best find in the Klondike to date. Carmack said he had dealt himself "a Royal Flush in the game of life and the whole world was a Jackpot!" Rabbit Creek became Bonanza Creek and the Gold Rush was on (10). Henderson was only on the other side of the mountain but so isolated that he didn't learn of the fabulous strike on Bonanza until it was too late. The friends made their discovery on August 16, 1896, and by September there were about 500 prospectors in the area. August 16th is celebrated as

"Discovery Days". A fork of Bonanza was even richer and became Eldorado Creek. Forty claims on Eldorado yielded a million dollars each. Claim 30 on Bonanza was thought to be useless and was sold to Big Alex MacDonald for a sack of flour and a side of bacon. It became the richest prospect yielding 5,000 dollars a day! There are many interesting stories about those claims but the one I like most concerns Commissioner Ogilvie. The miners felt that some of the claims were not properly staked. William Ogilvie surveyed each one and to his great credit satisfied all the miners. At the end 89 feet had not been registered and Ogilvie was too honest to claim it for himself!

In January, 1897, news of the strike reached Circle City, Alaska, and overnight it became a ghost town. Dawson City was named after Canadian geologist, George M. Dawson. It was situated near the claims where the Klondike River flows into the Yukon River. The townsite was created by Joe Ladue who also sold lots, whisky and dressed lumber. When 2 tons of gold reached Seattle in the summer of 1897, the mayor and many others quit their jobs to head north. Before Dawson became iced in for the winter of 1897 many more miners reached the Klondike. Others were marooned on Yukon River steamers, or had to wait at Lake Bennett. Dawson was not prepared for the influx of people and the population experienced serious food shortages before steamers arrived in June, 1898.

In the clammer for gold, riches and adventure many colourful people reached Dawson. Amongst them were Flora Shaw, foreign correspondent for the London Times (3), William Ogilvie who soon became Commissioner, diamond-toothed Gertie, Klondike Kate (I mean the Real Klondike Kate, Kathrine Ryan, based in Whitehorse, who would have been fascinating to meet (6)), the banker and poet Robert Service, Big Alex MacDonald (The King of the Klondike) (10), the author of "Call of the Wild" and "White Fang " Jack London, and Sam Steele.

Samuel Benfield Steele had just completed a successful man hunt in south-western Alberta (38). Colonel Steele of the Northwest Mounted Police, NWMP, was ordered to go north in January, 1898. Arriving in Skagway in February he commented that it was the "roughest place in the world." Soapy Smith and his gang robbed and sometimes murdered anyone except the Mounties. He reached the top of the Chilkoot Pass in time to open the customs house, raise the Union Jack and establish the Canadian boundary. Most of the miners were American and not pleased to meet the firm control taken by Steele and his company. Attempts were made to move the boundary further east but Maxim machine guns at the customs house and the iron rule of Steele soon became accepted. On the White and Chilkoot Passes the Mounties collected a tax, took charge of guns, and checked that each prospector was properly provisioned. Only then, were they allowed to proceed to Lake Bennett where they camped and built boats. The Argonauts soon discovered that the Mounties were also compassionate people giving advice about boat construction and sorting out squabbles where possible. Where some partners could not be reconciled, pans, boats and tents were sometimes cut in half! The Mounties were known to have provided blankets, money, sled dogs and tents to people in distress. One blushing bride appeared before Steele in an officer's scarlet tunic after she had fallen through the ice! A banker asked Steele to take care of $2 million to establish a bank in Dawson (19). He put it all under his bed, probably the largest stash ever hidden under the mattress. Steele made up some of the rules as the Johnnie on the spot.

All boats were numbered and documented so they could be checked through the rapids to make sure there were none missing.

Each person had to have 318 kilograms of food due to the shortage in Dawson. He described the site on May 29th, 1898, when the huge flotilla started to sail down Lake Bennett: "The wonderful exodus of boats began. I went up the hill behind the office to see the start and at one time counted 800 boats under sail in the eleven and a half miles of Lake Bennett." With all the precautions taken there were still 150 boat wrecks on the first day and 5 people drowned! At Myles Canyon, Steele put a corporal in charge to make sure each boat had a competant steersman, each boat had sufficient freeboard in the corporal's judgment and all women and children had to walk the 8 km. One Kitty Rockwell (who became the second Klondike Kate (3)) thought this rule to be against the rights of women and dressed as a boy, slipped aboard when the Mountie's back was turned. Later she confessed it was a very scary ride and wished she had taken Steele's advice.

In September Steele took charge of all the Mounties in the Yukon and British Columbia. The people of Dawson City quickly took him to their hearts. No one was allowed to carry a gun, the law ruled, and the streets were safe. Dangerous Dan McGrew could not have shot it out over "the favours of the lady known as Lou." Steele had estabished at the end of 1898 that the crime statistics for Dawson City would have compared favourably with any community in the Empire. The Mounties (38) were tough but the gambling houses were allowed to operate 6 days a week, 24 hours a day. Gambling was illegal in Canada, but again, it shows Steele's compassion and his understanding of the miners needs.

A mailman wrote, "They handle the situation not by brute force, which would have been a physical impossibility, but by common sense, tact and fearlessness." (10) The Sabbath was a different matter; no work was allowed.

TRAVELLING THE DEMPSTER

Steele had many responsibilities: head of the Mounties, Chairman of the Board of Health and Magistrate. When Steele arrived, Dawson was a swampy sewer with no clean water and people dying of typhoid fever. He quickly organised a water system and drainage ditches. Prisoners were organised to collect slops with a sanitary cart from each cabin . Big Sam was an interesting magistrate. Gamblers, pimps and confidence men could simply have been banished from the territory for an offence. Those who refused to leave would probably get 6 months hard labour. Steele's special pride and joy was the infamous Dawson woodpile. The thousands of cords of wood were stacked up in a pile often more than 3 km. long! It was used to heat all the government buildings. Fifty or more Dawson toughs were kept busy 10 hours a day. One imaginative convict got his revenge by sawing all the logs just one centimeter too long for the wood stoves! The heavy fines levied as magistrate and police chief were transferred to the health board for the care of patients. The Commissioner's federal funds were not nearly enough. One apocryphal story has Steele fineing a gambler 50 dollars "Oh, is that all? I've got that in my vest pocket," says the gambler. "And 60 days on the woodpile? Have you got that in your vest?" says Steele. As Licencing Officer he was able to raise $90,000 for the territorial coffers which prevented the Yukon from going bankrupt.

The gambling saloons were allowed to operate quite openly providing there was no cheating. Officers were always looking over gamblers' shoulders. If anyone complained they were immediately re-imbersed, because Steele's punishment would be 3 months on the dreaded woodpile! In Steele country disparaging remarks against Royalty was unacceptable and one comedian left the courtroom agreeing to sin no more! In booming Dawson everything shut down precisely at midnight on Saturday. No one who was there forgot the quiet Sunday atmosphere.

Big Sam commanded enormous respect from the Dawsonites and the surrounding camps. The Mounties earned $1.25 a day which was less than a labouring miner might earn. Yet these dedicated men stayed loyal to their calling in the Yukon Territory. Sam Steele was a Conservative and his boss, Minister Clifford Sifton, was a Liberal. Sifton's constant appointment of government officials to the area eventually caused too much conflict between himself and Steele. These people extracted too much graft from the miners, which Steele could not tolerate. Of the 6 members of the Yukon Council only Commissioner Ogilvie and Steele were not making money on the side (10).

Sifton notified Steele his duties were terminated in September 1899. Steele tried to keep it quiet but the community was outraged and protested in vain. He was scheduled to leave on September 26th and people from kilometers around gathered to see him off. Big Alex MacDonald was appointed to speak for the crowd. At that emotional moment Big Alex's power of speech failed him: "Here Sam, here ye are, poke for ye an goodbye." (10) Even when the steamer carrying Steele had passed out of sight the cheering for their hero could still be heard. I first became aware of Sam Steele after visiting Fort Steele where Wild Horse Creek flows into the Kootenay River in southern British Columbia. Of all the tributes, perhaps Mount Steele, Canada's 6th highest mountain is most appropriate. He was a pillar of strength in the Yukon, and again later in the Boer War. During the 1st World War Steele was knighted and made a General. He received many deserved accolades except the one he most wanted: Commissioner of his beloved NWMP (38).

For a short three years Dawson and the Yukon represented adventure, freedom and for a few wealth. As Robert Service put it:

"the north has got him." The north captured the hearts and minds of many including ourselves a century later. It is estimated that between 1885 and 1927, 127 million dollars worth of gold was removed from the Klondike (19). After 1901 companies began to replace placer mining or goldpanning. It was men like Joe Boyle who became the second wave of successful entrepreneurs. He had organised the petition to keep Sam Steele in the Yukon. Boyle fashioned the future of the Klondike: moving into concession mining, bringing in huge dredges to replace hand mining, developing hydro power for his machines and providing electric lights for the homes and commercial quarter of Dawson (40). The North Fork Ditch Road is still accessible where Boyle's hydroelectric plant produced power for the dredges and lights of Dawson. He managed a hockey team, the Klondike Nuggets, who went to Ottawa to play in an early Stanley Cup Final. He financed a

Joe Boyle Dawson City Museum and Historical Society Photo #984.136.3

corp of fighting men to support the Empire in the 1st World War. The editor of Dawson Daily News wrote "Unbounded credit is due to Joseph Whiteside Boyle for his more than generous contribution, which makes it possible for the Yukon to have a brigade in the great conflict." (40) He was believed to have been the lover of Romania's beautiful Queen Marie, his greatest and last love.

JOHN NEVILLE

We stayed at Bonanza Gold RV Park for the night. The famous creek rushed and swirled with muddy meltwater. Where we stood, the inside bend of the creek was undercutting the bank. Falco stood a little too close to the edge. The bank gave way, leaving Falco on his belly and two front paws dangling just above the water. Higher up the creek a huge derelict dredge stands like a dinosaur from the Industrial Age with its feet in the water. Our last stop was at the Tintina Bakery for coffee and delicious homemade pastries!

In the middle of June we decided to pay one more visit to Dawson. Our first stop was at the Museum to discuss a few photographs for this volume. Then we went to explore some of the exhibits before watching the film "City Of Gold", which was worth the price of admission alone. Pierre Burton did a very nice job narrating the history of Dawson City, his home town. Being a nature recordist I couldn't help noticing that Pierre Burton's narration was made on tape which hissed, while the film music was a higher quality recording. Klondike Kate's restaurant was like a siren calling us back for good food. We sat out on the patio in shirt sleeves enjoying the good weather and delicious desserts. Having a night on the town was not yet over: we went on to the Grand Palace to be entertained. The show was, of course, about the 1898 era and was good fun but not great. In true small theatre fashion the person selling the tickets also had the leading lady's part.

For me the highlight of our return trip to Dawson came the next morning. After some inquiries we headed to Eighth Street and the Jack London cabin. However, it was not really Jack London but the curator, Dick North (32,33), whom I wanted to meet. He's getting on in years but has a very sharp mind. He led us around the photographs, the copy of London's gold claim and much more. Many years ago, after some detective work he had located Jack London's original cabin on the Stewart River. After arranging to bring it to Dawson in

TRAVELLING THE DEMPSTER

the 1960's he managed to avoid an incident with the California Jack London Society. With some assistance, he explained that they rebuilt two cabins with half of the original logs in each. One of the tiny cabins is on Eighth Street and the other was delivered to Oakland where the Jack London Society is based. My primary interest was Dick's own books about the Mad Trapper and the Lost Patrol, and another twenty minutes quickly went by. I happened to mention Joe Boyle and Dick related further research. He had corresponded with Queen Marie's eldest daughter before she died. An hour had quickly slipped by and only then did more people start to arrive. We quickly got our copy of Trackdown autographed and sadly bid farewell to a very interesting Dawson citizen. The last thing he mentioned was his Mad Trapper talks which would commence as soon as the basketball playoffs were over.

CHAPTER 2

THE BOREAL FOREST:
KILOMETERS 0 TO 72

*Including: Tintina Trench, Boreal Forest, Beringia, Taiga,
Lynx and Snowshoe Hare, Voles, History of the Dempster and
Tombstone Campground*

Forty kilometers east of Dawson we turned off the Klondike Highway. At 4 pm, May 11th we began the journey northeast along the Dempster Highway. The elevation was 446 m. and the temperature was a balmy 20 degrees C. Our Global Positioning System (GPS) registered North 63 degrees (') 59 minutes (") and West 138'44". The irradescent green and blue of Violet-green Swallows greeted us crossing the Klondike River. They chatter constantly in the sky while hawking for insects. The road enters the Tintina Trench and follows the North Klondike River enveloped by the Boreal Forest. The trench is a major geological fault that extends from the Rocky Mountain Trench in British Columbia, northwest across the Yukon and into Alaska. It marks an ancient collision point between North America and drifting fragments of other continents. About 65 million years ago Ross River and Dawson City would have been opposite to each other but are now several hundred kilometers apart.

For two years in the springtime we have been birding in the boreal forest from Manitoba, across Saskatchewan and Alberta to northern B.C. and the Northwest Territories. This year of 2004 in the Yukon Territory we are again in muskeg with Black Spruce, tall White Spruce, Aspen, Cottonwood (Balsam Poplar), Willow and Birch. Evidence of glaciation is obvious in the mountains but the Trench remained more or less ice free during the last ice age. One glacier moved down from the Tombstone Range, only partially blocking the valley, near the present day Tombstone Campground.

The area was quite cold but most of the Pacific moisture fell on the coastal mountains preventing a build up of snow and ice. People crossing the Bering Landbridge were able to funnel southward between ice sheets and follow other mammals and birds for food. In the refuge that we call Beringia, Calef (12) describes:

"Mastadons, Woolly Mammoths, Camels, Wild Horses, Large Horned Bison, Lions, Saiga Antelope, Ground Sloth, and Giant Beavers the size of Bears".

Imagine if we could see those critters today as we drive along! The Old Crow Flats and the Dawson gravel beds have turned up many bones and fossils. Escaping from glaciation also allowed gold to collect in gravel beds and lodge in bedrock causing the rush of rushes 100 years ago. Before entering each new region of the road we refer to George Calef's (12) and Robert Frisch's (18) books to gain insight. Frisch divides this region into two zones:

1. Boreal Forest with overlapping canopies to kilometer 50.

2. Taiga where the trees diminish in size as the elevation increases (elevation 673 meters). This subalpine forest is sometimes called the Taiga, which is Frisch's second zone. There are no trails in this area so walking off the road is difficult. Mountain Spruce appear with patches of talus and tundra, separating clumps

of willow and birch. At kilometer 54 we turned west on a road leading to a microwave tower. A screaming call drew our attention to a Merlin perched in the spire of a spruce. Checking him out in our books he was appropriately defined as the Taiga form because of his gray and white colouring.

Treeline is officially at 68 km. and an elevation of 1,070 m.

Arctic Hare

As we passed the boundary, it was even more clearly defined by a large cinnamon grizzly, running across the road and disappearing into some scrub. This line of changing vegetation also approximates to the edge of permafrost (permanently frozen ground). At lower elevations the treeline extends north all the way to the estuaries of the Yukon and Mackenzie Rivers. Because there are trees in the Mackenzie River valley we will only see tundra in the Ogilvie and Richardson Mountains, parts of Eagle Plain and Peel Plateau.

At the beginning of March, Heather got an email from the producer of CBC "The Nature of Things". The message kindly informed us of a program called "The Ghost Walker" on March 17th. We sat down to watch biologist Liz Hofer studying Lynx and their relationship to Snowshoe Hare (39). The study area is southwest of us but still in Yukon's Boreal Forest. This patient biologist has been studying these animals since 1986 near Kluane

National Park. Suddenly, I became aware of the bird calls, such as a Common Raven, and remembered that they were my recordings being used to create the soundscape. The Wildcat, Bobcat, Ghost Walker or Lynx's favourite dish is one hare a day. The familiar voice of David Suzuki tells us that this drama is played out in Canada's Boreal Forest, the largest remaining forest on the planet. The lynx has very keen eye-sight, being able to spot a hare at 300 m. and can make large jumps. The hare has a keen sense of smell and can run at 50 kph., which is 20 kph. faster than the lynx. We clocked one, even faster, at 60 kph. on the Klondike Highway! The predator must ambush its dinner and use its 4 m. leap to make contact. Liz Hofer was shown carefully tracking and making notes.

The hare population peaks every 10 years at about 4 animals per hectare. The last peak was in 1998, but only 3 years later had crashed to 1 critter per 25 hectares! The Hudson's Bay Company records for the last two hundred years indicate peaks in the hare population. The name 'snowshoe' comes from the large hind feet measuring up to 7.5 cm. in length with wide spreading toes and a thick covering of stiff hairs. These animals are easily trapped along their runways and are still used for food and clothing by the northern people. When hare become scarce, many lynx starve to death and others move to better hunting grounds. In the low parts of the hare cycle they become, as Suzuki puts it, "Just a dream in the lynx mind". At those times a flock of raven might alert the lynx to a wolf kill. Unfortunately the lynx is not well adapted for eating frozen meat.

The hare browse on willow and birch but with its strong sense of smell, it can find twigs when they are covered in snow. The tufts of hair next to the lynx ears and its whiskers are very sensitive to wind direction. This assists in careful planning of ambush positions, downwind of the hare. The large frame and dense fur causes the lynx to look much larger than its maximum 16 kilos. The usual walking speed of the lynx is only about 1 kph., and it may stop to snooze several times a day. When out tracking, Liz Hofer must be careful not to overtake the animal as she would cause it to behave unnaturally. The camera zooms in on a patch of ice where the animal has lain in wait for a squirrel. There was a small mound of snow hiding the lynx from the squirrel's midden but the lucky squirrel did not make a fateful trip to the cached nuts. The tracks show the lynx eventually moving on. The snow leaves some fascinating stories: a female lynx made 32 unsuccessful jumps to catch a hare. Liz explains that it was a lot of energy to use up but it was also a time of scarce food.

Once upon a time, our ancestors were good trackers in order to survive. Liz Hofer has relearned these skills to gain knowledge about the interdependence of animals in the Boreal Forest. If the temperature drops below -30 degrees C the hare might seek shelter under a spruce. The lynx loses heat lying in the snow and must balance its need for food with the loss of energy to the cold. So far the observations have taken 18 years, painstakingly building up a story of hare and lynx. When only tracks are seen, the tracker sometimes has a sense of "walking with ghosts" as it were. The effect of predators on the Snowshoe Hare is to cause great stress particularly at the high point in the hare cycle. The female fertility goes down and her ability to raise her young, or leverets, diminishes. This stress may carry over into several generations curbing the total number of hares. The hare is a keystone species for the forest and the tundra further north. At the peak of the cycle the total biological mass of hare is greater than caribou or moose and has a huge effect on predators like lynx and large owls.

Travelling the Dempster

Mice, vole and lemmings are alternates for the lynx but the best years are when the hare are plentiful. Another interesting link in the web of lifeforms is the vole's cyclical pattern. The vole peak comes about 2 years after the hare. Hare droppings provide fertilizer for berry plants which in turn feed the smaller mammals. The voles can and do provide food for hungry lynx and wolves. One biologist observed a lynx catch 13 voles on 19 attempts. However, it takes about 50 voles to equal 1 hare. This would be about 4 hours of constant mousing, a lot of energy to put out for the lynx. In springtime, the snow melts and all the endless tracks disappear preventing Liz Hofer from following till next fall. As the hares shed winter coats for sleaker brown fashions, the biologists put their records in order and people like us come along with MiniDisc recorders and cameras. To date my closest encounter with a lynx came at Pine Lake in Wood Buffalo National Park, 2 years ago. I was standing quite still at dawn waiting to record Common Loon, and heard a purring sound behind me, assuming it was a feral cat. I was concentrating on loon sounds and therefore did not turn to record or identify the newcomer. Heather was standing some distance away and enjoyed a good look at the lynx before it slipped away into the woods.

In northern mythology the Snowshoe Hare was a witchdoctor. In Africa, the hare was a bright lively mythological character. The slaves brought those stories to North America in the form of Brer Rabbit. As a boy in England I loved those stories, as do my children. Peter Rabbit is another endearing character of many peoples' childhood. On our journey along the Dempster the only place that Snowshoe Hare was abundant was between kilometers 110 and 112, six years after a cyclical peak. Walking to stretch our legs one afternoon a curious thing happened. A hare sat quite still as we passed but could not quite keep his nerve when Falco walked by. The hare took off for a willow thicket. Falco, our dog, is firmly disciplined not to chase wildlife and on this trip not to leave the gravel road. However, this particular incident was too much for him and he was off in hot pursuit. The rabbit zigged and zagged through three thickets bounding at a fast rate. Falco took a fairly direct route through the first thicket, but lost the scent before entering the second. He quartered back and forth scenting, looking and listening. Meantime Brer Rabbit had appeared about 25 m. away on the road. He amazed us by sitting down in the road where he could watch us and Falco searching amongst the willows. Was he just curious, did he enjoy a chase, or did he have a sense of humour and was laughing at us?

As we drove along I reflected on some of the history behind this 28 m. ribbon of gravel. The creation of the Dempster was part of a political platform to increase development in Northern Canada. It is Canada's only public highway north of the Arctic Circle that is open year round, excepting winter blizzards, break-up and freeze-up. It was part of the Roads to Resources platform of the Conservative minority government of 1957. There was some prospect of oil in the Eagle Plains region so the idea was not entirely altruistic. It was embraced as part of John Diefenbaker's ambitious vision of the north that became a key factor in his re-election by a huge majority in 1958. The Liberal criticism that it was a road from "igloo to igloo" fell on deaf ears. In 1959, the first 48 km. were built. For the next two years only another 77 km. were added at a lower grade with a diminishing budget. Because so little of the geography was known, surveying was done with aircraft, followed by more detailed work in helicopters. For seven years construction ceased altogether.

Then in 1969, a Liberal Government provided more funds and an improved design. With the discovery of oil and gas at Prudo

Bay, Alaskan pressure to complete the Dempster increased. Its first section was called Yukon Territorial Road #11, changing to Flat Creek Road, then Eagle Plain Road and finally at its northern end Aklavik Road. It was a while before the name Dempster Highway, after Corporal Jack Dempster of NWMP, was adopted. Later in this year of 2004, August 18th, a party was planned to mark the 25th Anniversary of the opening of this amazing road.

When we reached kilometer 7 we turned off to explore a side road. There was an old burn site towards the Klondike River, a small creek and lots of moose poop. It was late afternoon so the birds were quiet, even the Robins. Taking a walk we became aware of a barking dog but no houses. Suddenly a young woman and her dog appeared. Her voice sounded familiar so I asked if her name was Julie. I had spoken to Julie Frisch, a Dempster naturalist and wife of the late Robert Frisch, on

Inspector W.J.Dempster
photo Eagle Plains Hotel

the phone recently. The response came "No, but she's my mum."

We had a good chat and met Julie in the evening. Julie had a beautiful cabin nearby on the edge of the Klondike River. We traded birding stories,and birding friends late into the evening at her picnic table. Julie also added to our pile of books and articles in the Bird Mobile. The next morning we heard a beautiful melody whistled by a Fox Sparrow. It was raining so we planned to return to record it later. However, the weather improved a little and I was able to make a good recording of a Ruby-crowned Kinglet at kilometer 32. From kilometer 40 the road climbed steadily towards a magical kingdom of snow covered peaks in the Ogilvie Mountains. At about 7:30 pm we pulled into the Tombstone Campground for the night surrounded by the mountains and the last stand of trees at timberline. Our GPS registered 1,048 m. elevation. To the west of us, Mount Monolith rises to a sharp peak and somewhere beyond it is the Tombstone Mountain. We stopped by the Interpretive Center as all the campsites were still buried under .5 m. of snow. Heather cooked some fresh halibut that she bought in Dawson. Eating the meal in such a wonderful setting we appreciated our good fortune snug in the Bird Mobile.

CHAPTER 3

THE SOUTHERN OGILVIES:
KILOMETERS 72 TO 132.

Including: Tombstone Mountain, Our first Tundra, Willow
Ptarmigan, Woodland Caribou, Semipalmated Plover,
the Lost Patrol, Two Moose Lake and Gray Jays.

A short walk outside the campground in the morning allowed me to focus a microphone on the Fox Sparrow's melodious song and make a pleasing recording. Willow Ptarmigan were below the road but not quite close enough to record. A White-crowned Sparrow did come close enough but the noise of a cold wind spoilt the moment.

This region is a harsh mountain landscape with rolling tundra uplands. The Southern Ogilvie mountain range was sculpted by glaciation and the carved features and rockie detritus are very evident. Our first stop was at kilometer 74, a viewpoint for Tombstone Mountain. The spectacular peaks of the Tombstones were exposed as the sedimentary rock was eroded away. Sadly, the Tombstone Mountain peak was shaded in cloud but many of the other mountains were in full sunshine. The wedge-shaped peak was an important reference point for the Mounties and trappers. At the height of the ice age, the Tombstone glacier flowed down to the big bend of the North Klondike River. The undulating landscape in the valley bottom today marks the terminal moraine of that glacier, including the Tombstone Campground. The road lead us into the North Fork Pass surrounded by mountains with flat tundra to either side. The Finnish word "tunturi" means treeless plain. The North Fork Pass ascends from kilometer 72 to 87. The high point comes at kilometer 81, at 1,134 m. which is also a continental divide. There are rich meadows and heath punctuated by scree, talus and rocky outcrops, and the pass forms a watershed between the Pacific and Arctic drainages. Heather marvelled out loud at the forces that created and sculpted this landscape. The flora is mainly scrub birch and willow, with itermittant bare tussock, tundra and fen. I was delighted to find so many Willow Ptarmigan, and several stayed close to the road to be recorded. Grouse and ptarmigan are the chicken-like (Gallinaceous) birds

Willow Ptarmigan photot by Norman Barichello

of the Boreal and Arctic regions. In the winter they may be the only birds for many kilometers on the tundra. The Latin name for the ptarmigan is Lagapus meaning rabbit's foot because their feet are fully feathered. This feature provides insulation and allows them to walk easily on soft snow. The Rock Ptarmigan is just called the Ptarmigan in Europe and is circumpolar in the Arctic region. The Willow Ptarmigan likes riparian land where willow buds provide good winter browse. In Scotland they are a popular gamebird called Red Grouse. As we drive along, the male ptarmigan often stand on the road attempting to protect their territory. Only the silhouette of a circling eagle makes them disperse quickly. Willow Ptarmigan and American Tree Sparrows are common sights and sounds throughout this region. Lans, in his book Along The Dempster (25), describes many climbing opportunities in this area.

At kilometer 75 an abandoned road heads up the west fork of the Hart River. The Woodland Caribou of Hart Mountain stay near this part of the Dempster Highway year round. Just like there are Killer Whales with separate pods and very distinctive behaviour patterns, so it is with caribou. There are about 1,500 animals in this herd which range up and down the Hart and Blackstone drainages. These caribou move up and down in response to the season without making the long migration typical of the Barren Ground Caribou herds further north. The calves of Woodland Caribou are born above the treeline in brushy canyons or open ridges. The animals remain in the high mountains during the summer, seeking relief from mosquitoes on snow patches or wind swept ridges and feeding on lush new plant growth. When the snow begins to fall the herd starts descending into the forested valleys. Woodland Caribou may be spotted from the Highway near the West Hart River in the summer and autumn. About ten years ago we were crossing the Selkirk Mountains in southern B.C. on Highway #3, aka. Kootenay Pass. We pulled into the Summit Lake carpark late on a January afternoon. The road was covered with a thin layer of ice making driving quite treacherous. Visibility was down to about 10 m. so we stopped for a rest and hoped the weather conditions would improve. Suddenly, there were four Woodland Caribou moving around the car with antlers more than a meter across and wearing tracking collars. Almost as quickly as they came, their ghostly forms disappeared back into the mist. I quickly wound the window down and could hear the sound of their clicking heel bones as they moved away. That particular herd now is in decline with fewer than 40 animals and is the only caribou herd crossing into the lower 48 States. A man calling himself a hunter shot one of those protected animals that winter and took it home. He was surprised when he pulled into his driveway because a game warden drove in behind him. The foolish man had omitted to remove the tracking collar!

Descending from the North Fork Pass, another distinct zone begins at kilometer 87 called the Blackstone Uplands. The road follows the river and passes many lakes and ponds. Weather patterns from the west and north meet here causing summer storms and about 35 cm. of precipitation. It is the wettest part of the highway. Willow thickets flourish along the river banks. Nearby glacial moraines provided the gravel for this part of the road. At Kilometer 91, an outfitters' cabin has been built next to a shallow pond and the Blackstone River. This proved good for recording. The sun was out and the one negative factor was a cool wind. On the pond Mallard, American Widgeon and Northern Pintails were swimming in their breeding plumage. The Mallards were noisiest. Near the cabin a large flock of Lapland Longspur were feeding on seed and horse droppings. Their high peeping sounds and tee-tle calls were first time recordings for me. Most of the river was covered with ice. Standing on the ice and resting, or feeding, were a flock of Mew Gulls. When they took off and circled low overhead the leader's calls were urgent, demanding to be followed. Returning two days later we found the scene had changed. The fast flowing water was constantly grinding up the remaining ice. The Lapland Longspur had been replaced by two male birds circling back and forth, sometimes doubling back on themselves. They had bold colouring: brown back, black and white collar and yellow legs. They called and trilled loudly, circling around and over my head. While I stood very still making two extensive recordings, Heather got out the bird books to confirm that they were

TRAVELLING THE DEMPSTER

Semipalmated Plovers.

At kilometer 98 a broad expanse of tundra opened up to the left. Three Woodland Caribou moved away from the road. After 100 m. or so they turned and stood quite still, like statues, watching the Bird Mobile pass. Heather readied her camera but the animals were too distant for a good photograph. At kilometer 108 we encountered road construction signs. The Blackstone was quickly eroding its bank close to the highway. The Highway's crew were all sitting in their trucks when we passed, presumably contemplating the problem. This section of highway was also the roughest so far and was badly in need of grading. Between kilometers 115 and 117, the road crosses the old NWMP dogsled trail. An informative tribute commemorates the patrols near Chapman Lake. The McPherson Patrols took place from 1904 to 1921 with only one tragedy- the death of the members of the Lost Patrol (13) in 1911. Unlike other trips the Lost Patrol began from Fort McPherson instead of Dawson. The four men and 21 dogs mushed out of McPherson on December 21, 1910, led by Inspector Francis J.Fitsgerald. The three sleds contained 590 kilograms of supplies, 400 of which were fish for the dogs. This was calculated to last them 30 days. The 750 km. journey should have taken less than a month! Deep snow strong winds and intense cold, at times reaching -65 degrees C., plagued the travellers from the start. It's hard to imagine the harsh conditions those men struggled through, but I can recall the weather forecast nearly every day last January: "Blizzards on the Dempster". On Boxing Day they met several Gwitchen families, discovered they had taken a wrong turn and hired Essau George to guide them to the Peel River. Unfortunately they dismissed their guide after only five days. It was a fateful decision not to ask Essau George to guide them the rest of the way! After 19 days on the trail Fitsgerald had only reached the headwaters of the Little Wind

River, 400 km. from McPherson. There they looked for the trail that would take them over the Hart Divide. Their guide was an Ex-Mountie, Sam Carter, but he had only taken the route once before, and that was in the opposite direction. They looked without success for another 7 days.

Then they made a desperate dash back towards McPherson but their tracks had been obliterated by moving snow. By February 1st, they had eaten 8 of their dogs and the weather continued stormy and bitterly cold! Fitsgerald noted, "Skin peeling off our faces and parts of the body". On February 5th Fitsgerald made his last entry noting that he had fallen through river ice and frozen a foot, and they only had 5 dogs left. When officers Taylor and Kenny could go no further, a shelter was made for them. Taylor took his own life when the end was near. About 16 kilometers further on first Carter then Fitsgerald died, only 40 kilometers from Fort McPherson.

Essau George and some companions reached Dawson on February 20th and reported that they had met and helped Fitsgerald, who was lost, on December 26th. The police became alarmed and dispatched Corporal Jack Dempster to find the missing patrol. One of the keys to this search was the employment of a competent first nation guide, Charlie Stewart. Fighting very difficult conditions, Dempster did not pick up their trail till March 12th. Ten days later he found the bodies of Fitsgerald and his companions. The bodies were taken to McPherson for burial. If they had taken more supplies and a Gwitchen guide who knew the trail, despite the brutal weather, the tragedy might not have happened. The dye was cast when Essau George was dismissed. Sam Carter insisted that he knew the route which is perhaps the primary reason for the tragedy. They took a rifle, but no shotgun. A shotgun would have allowed them to kill small game and stay alive long enough to reach Fort McPherson. A high powered rifle was next to useless for killing small game. Pride or over confidence precluded them using a local native guide—a big mistake which cost them their lives. The mistakes of Sir John Franklin had still not been fully heeded.

On the bank of the Great Slave River near Fort Smith is a tiny community called Fort Fitsgerald which keeps the name of the Lost Patrol leader alive in our memories. Laura Burton in I Married the Klondike (9) reported the sad news reaching Dawson, while she was at a dinner party at Government House. Dempster remained in the Yukon to make more dog sled patrols between Dawson and McPherson than any other Mountie, establishing speed records in both directions. The patrols often continued north to Herschel Island to deliver the mail to the mission and the whaling community.

Dog Sleds Dawson City Museum and Historical Society Photo#9894.761.181

That evening found us camped on the bank of the Blackstone River. A passing motorist stopped to caution us that he had seen a large grizzly moving up the valley towards us about a half kilometer away. We took his warning seriously and did not go out that evening. We saw or heard no sign of the bear. The following morning I was on the road at about 7 am with two sweaters, a coat and gloves. My brain was not fully alert but the heavy silence of the north was all about me. If Thoreau had walked this way he might have made far-reaching observations. In my case, it was a endless sense of wonder, having the wilderness all about me. It was a long cold morning's walk with not much to show for the effort. I recorded one robin out on the tundra. However, the walk was enjoyable, with the open tundra on one side and the Blackstone River on the other. The temperature was 2 degrees C when I set out. As the temperature rose I peeled my coat and outer sweater. The temperature continued to climb till 9pm when it reached 22 degrees C. The afternoon was far more productive: an American Wigeon, a Lesser Yellowlegs and most exciting an Upland Sandpiper allowed their voices to be imprinted on minidisc. The song of the sandpiper is a melodic series of whistles and trills that becomes unforgetable to the listener. Walking slowly for about 10 km. is quite tiring but those three birds certainly made it worthwhile.

Because the Blackstone Valley is so rich in birdlife we decided to return to Two Moose Lake at 102 km for the night. A beautiful platform has been constructed to overlook the lake. We parked with our door only 1 m. from the platform. In effect we had a very attractive deck for the evening. The lake itself was still mainly frozen. The ice was beginning to decay with open water at its edges. The odd fish jumped. We sat out first drinking a glass of Chardonnay and later our coffee. There was no wind, the sunniest evening I've ever known at 10 o'clock. Only two vehicles passed us. It's hard to express the feeling of tranquility we were both feeling. The silence of the north actually seems to hum when you listen to it. I imagine it's the sound of the world spinning and that night Heather noticed it too.

The next day at about kilometer 124 noisy jays began to call as soon as the Bird Mobile came to a stop. We decided to offer the Camp Robbers aka Whisky Jacks, aka Gray Jays some vegetables and seed. The effect was immediate and a family of five jays swarmed in for an afternoon snack. The sounds of the persistent youngsters were loud and raucous! The adult male positioned himself on our roof and first the female then the young jays came swooping in near my feet. After recording for several minutes I decided to stop throwing out the food and simply held it out in my hand. Both adults would move in and by turn land on my hand exploring the texture of my fingers with their claws. Usually and quite delicately one large piece of food would be selected and taken away for consumption. One youngster landed on the parabola but did not risk my hand. The adults are a light gray with a darker head and mask. The three young birds were a darker gray and a darker bill.

The noise made by these five attracted another family of four jays. The second family quickly moved from the periphery to where the food was. However, the first male began to call with some variations establishing himself and his family as having prior rights. He did a perfect imitation of a Merlin, to my ear. The other family did not fly away but were definitely cowed by the versatile performance of the dominant male. The raucous sounds also brought a Common Raven, one Three-toed Woodpecker, a Ruby-crowned Kinglet and a real Merlin to the scene. The Merlin passed through at 75 kilometers an hour or thereabouts. All in all, the jays were well fed. Heather got some close-up photographs and the MiniDisc Recorder absorbed about 10 minutes of electronic data.

CHAPTER 4

THE NORTHERN OGILVIES:
KILOMETERS 132 TO 248

*Including: Beaver, Windy Pass, Gyrfalcon,
Geophony, and Flooding River*

As we left the Blackstone Uplands at kilometer 132 we were approaching a narrow valley in the mountains. The GPS read North 64 degrees ' 57 minutes ", West 138'14", altitude 928 m. Our direction was only 5 degrees west of north. George Calef (12) described this landscape as: "rolling mountains and hills composed largely of sedimentary rock, such as limestone, dolamite and shale, which account for the light gray colour of the mountains when seen from a distance". Rubble and scree are very evident but the changes are due to erosion not glaciation. Some ridges have been carved into towers and pinnacles called ramparts or castellations due to the effects of wind and water.

The highway remained in forested valleys. Tamarack trees appeared for the first time joining White Spruce and cottonwoods along the rivers. Calef (12) mentions some rare plants living in these mountains which pre-date the last ice age. The ascending road was just below treeline so the trees were typical taiga or subalpine in stature. The Ogilvie Mountains, which towered above, were named for the first white man to describe them, William Ogilvie, who appeared in Chapter 1.

Travelling the Dempster

Entering Windy Pass we stopped with a pond to our left, up against a cliff. I was able to record the peeping sounds of Green-winged Teal with a gentle tinkling sound of running water in the background. At kilometer 144 there were the remains of a beaver dam on the east side of the road. Most beaver do not build dams in the north because of the lack of suitable trees, but create dens in river banks where willows and poplar provide food. We saw our first one at Two Moose Lake.

Peter C. Newman calls them: "the pugnosed rodent with the lustrous fur" (31). Fur trapping and trading began slowly in the 16th century. One hundred years later beaver hats had become very fashionable and the hunt for the quiet little animal gradually moved further west. In 1662, Samuel Pepys boasted that he had paid 85 shillings for a new hat. His beaver topper was so precious that he had a rabbit model for bad weather! Newman in The Company of Adventurers (31) describes how the European nobility passed laws stating who could and couldn't wear fur clothing. Beaver hats were willed from father to son. It was the fine underhairs that provided the wonderfully soft felt for the hats. The beaver's undercoat is covered with tiny barbs which allow the downie fibers to be matted, beaten, then shellacked into a lustrous soft texture. Beaver became extinct in Britain during the 15th century, so the dye was cast for the North American fur trade. With supreme irony, one Indian Chief marvelled how the beaver trade does everything perfectly well: he makes us kettles, axes, knives, gives us drink and food without the trouble of cultivating the ground. One "Made Beaver" became the official currency for trading. The value of one prime adult beaver skin was used to barter for all other commodities. For example, two otter pelts or ten pounds of goose feathers were each worth one made beaver.

JOHN NEVILLE

Pear-shaped scent glands are located near the annus of the beaver. They contain a bitter brown substance called Castorium, better known to me as Castor Oil. I can remember my mother advancing on me with a bottle and spoon to improve my health. It had many magical healing qualities but tasted awful! Between 1808 and 1828 the HBC exported nearly 10 tons of Castorium from the Athabaska region alone! In 1823 a steel trap was invented which greatly helped trappers to catch the pugnosed rodent. The HBC Factor at Rupert House tamed one but it chewed through all of their furniture. So they decided to banish the little fellow to an island: it ate first through its cage, then through the bottom of the boat! They only just reached land before the boat was swamped.

I have often recorded beaver, especially the splosh sound made as an alarm signal with the tail. The tail is also a very effective rudder for swimming and when moving logs for dam construction. It also acts as a prop when sitting to chew wood. On this trip, I also managed to record the high pitched calls of a beaver kit before the adult sounded the alarm with a splosh of its tail. Many dams, one or more km. long, have been found. David Thompson noted one, 5 km. long and he was able to ride across it two horses abreast. The dams not only provide a home and protection but create modified waterways and meadows for the use of the beaver, waterfowl, fish, moose and many others.

Disturbing the ecosystem affects many elements of the wildlife population. For example, the re-introduction of the wolf in Yellowstone National Park has reduced the elk population, which in turn has allowed willows and other trees to recover along waterways. The returning alder, willow and birch have provided food for recovering beaver populations and shade for local fish. Its difficult for us to fully comprehend the interaction of so many species in the food chain.

TRAVELLING THE DEMPSTER

We pulled off the road at kilometer 154. It was still cold and windy in Windy Pass! This dry, sparcely vegetated landscape is similar to Beringia during the last ice age. People crossing the land bridge would have seen gray cliffs and scree, just as it appears today. The scree has been darkened by lichen. If the lichen is disturbed the rocks show through as nearly white. Using her binoculars, Heather was able to follow the white zig zag trails of sheep to the top of adjacent cliffs.

The following morning at kilometer 158 we searched the cliff to the south for a Gyrfalcon nest. Four guano streaks on the cliff suggested four different scrape sites in the recent past. The female was perched on a pinnacle of rock, her white throat and chest prominent with some dark markings on her chest and belly. Her head and back were dark gray classifying her as a gray morph Gyrfalcon. This largest of all falcons, measured about 55cm from head to tail. She

Gyrfalcon photo by Norman Barichello

called for about two minutes when I first focused the microphone, sounding somewhat like a Prairie Falcon. The bird impressed us further when she left the aerie to fly along the cliff rim. The falcon's flight was very fast and hugged the terrain like a stealth jet. Her powerful short wingbeats quickly took her beyond the range of Heather's binos. She was definitely ruler of her dolamite kingdom. Earlier we had seen one of her tastier subjects, a Rock Ptarmigan, still in white plumage in the low scrub at the edge of the road. Our Yukon birding book (1) informed us that there are about 750 pairs of breeding Gyrs in the Yukon and we had just seen and heard our first. On the opposite cliff, two Western Wood Pewees were also committed to my MiniDisc recorder.

Shortly afterwards we passed five Dall Sheep in a gully. They stopped to survey the Bird Mobile's passage. Their pace, single file up the cliff seemed leisurely in a zig zag course along the trail. Their sure-footedness and ease of ascent was quite impressive. Like the Gyrfalcon they were beautifully adapted to their environment.

When this land was Eastern Beringia, the ground would have been covered in grass and sedges. Only when the climate became warmer and wetter did willows, poplar and spruce move north into this area as it is today. Some ancient giant animals such as the Woolly Mammoth died out in Beringia. Their end may have been due to hunting by humans passing through. Other animals isolated in Beringia by the ice sheets evolved into new species such as Dall's Sheep and caribou. Some plants and animals still living in the Pass pre-date the last ice age. For example, Alaskan scientists have traced an ancient moth which still lives on the lichen. The female is flightless and therefore lays her eggs close to where she was born. Sitting in the Bird Mobile with the wind howling outside it's not difficult to imagine that earlier time.

After kilometer 166 the road followed Engineer Creek. Where Red Creek joined the flow, the water was stained red with iron oxide. The creek had recently flooded and washed out part of the road. A local crew was busy diking Red Creek and repairing the road. A very faint smell of sulphur came from the water but it was not strong enough to be offensive. Nearby sulphur springs contribute to the waterflow in this area. A narrow valley soon squeezes the road and creek close together. Taiga forest follows the creek and robins, juncos, thrushes and flickers can be seen and heard. The creek sound made it too noisy for recording. Bernie Krause in Wild Sounds (24) calls wind, water, ice, earthquakes, volcanos, etc. "Geophony", the sounds of earth and its elements. The sound of living creatures, except those of humans he calls "Biophony". The creek was an impressive geophony, all but drowning out the biophony of birds.

At kilometer 181 we passed a bright red rock on the left. Where the softer rock had been eroded, castellations like battlements had been formed at the top of the cliffs. At kilometer 184 the sulphorous aroma increased to a reasonable approximation of bad eggs! At the Engineer Creek Campground we stopped to empty our garbage and put a few liters of water into our tank. We heard a loud dispute, the harsh calls of a raven contrasting with the alarm sounds of a peregrine, several meters back in the woods. We had no means of knowing the cause, but speculated on the rights to a dead hare or ptarmigan. On a nearby cliff known as Sapper Hill, raven and peregrine are known to nest (1). At kilometer 196, a three arched bridge carried the road across the Ogilvie River. The river was high, swirling with large bobbing chunks of ice flowing to the Arctic Ocean.

This area is fascinating for anyone who is interested in geology. The Travelogue, that Julie Frisch had given us, mentions, "Protruding from the slopes of rubble are towers, spikes and minarets of dolomite. Known as tors, these features are the product of frost shattering. Tors are found only in unglaciated terrain." A rest area appeared at km 220 with a convenient dumpster. The river had swollen over its banks at this point turning the dumpster into an island. A pair of merganser were carried out into the main stream. After unsuccessfully swimming against the current they turned and were quickly swept downstream. At 237 km. there is usually an emergency airstrip paralleling the road, but today it was totally under water. This is the most northerly known nesting site for a pair of Great Gray Owls. We were becoming a little nervous as the water was lapping up onto the road in some places.

CHAPTER 5

EAGLE PLAINS:
KILOMETERS 248 TO 410

Including: Ogilvie Ridge, Beringia again, the song of Varied
Thrush, End Dumping, Eagle Plains Hotel, The Mad Trapper of
Rat River, Rough-legged Hawk
and the Arctic Circle

Eventually we decided to drive out of the flood plain onto much higher ground at kilometer 259. The road ascended 300 meters up an escarpment onto the Eagle Plains overlook. The GPS reading was North 65'47", West 137'46 ", elevation 884 m. Looking out from our campsite to the north the snowcapped Richardson Mountains were visible aproximately 180 km. away! The Ogilvie-Peel rivers curved away to the east toward their destiny with the Mackenzie River. A well-prepared lookout had been developed near the pinnacle of the Ogilvie Ridge. In addition to the magnificent views there were some informative panels about the geology of the area. I attempted to record a Horned Lark on the hillside above the road but the wind thwarted my efforts. The plain had been Eastern Beringia or Mammoth Steppe all the way to the top of the Richardson Mountains. Our route would take us across the plains and over the Richardsons to the north.

The Plateau still reaches the British Mountains to the northwest, (named by Franklin in 1826 [35]) the Arctic Ocean and, when the ice is set, Herschel Island. The pre-historic horse travelled north across Beringia and the land bridge to reach Asia before becoming extinct in the Americas. It returned only five hundred years ago with the Spaniards . Sandhill Cranes still fly across Beringia to Siberia each spring. Sadly, we just missed the spectacle of 200,000 cranes flying up the Tintina Trench in early May. We can only speculate whether these northerly migrations began when the Bering Sea dried out to create a land bridge. The road was leading us across land that has historically been occupied by the Gwitchen people.

Eagle Plains has a misleading name. It is a landscape of rolling hills, partially covered with stunted Black Spruce. Frisch (18) reports that it is the area least likely to see an eagle. We were perhaps lucky to have a Golden Eagle circle high above us on this part of the road. Norm, the tanker driver for the Eagle Plains Hotel, also reported seeing a Bald Eagle regularly at the Eagle River Bridge. The first part of this region was fabulous rolling tundra. Heather was able to photograph Franklin's Scorpionweed, a Porcupine (only four feet off the ground) and a Black Bear foraging at the side of the road. I was able to record Tree, Fox and White-crowned Sparrows. The interesting thing about all three species were the local distinct dialects, which I will utilize on the CD.

As we drove across the plain the sunny weather quickly changed to cloud, then rain and a storm. This pattern repeated itself at least twice. Strong winds would subside and back into blue skies. In one bright spell a Varied Thrush presented himself amongst Black Spruce. There were no other birds or noisy creeks to spoil his recording. I quickly setup, and recorded three or four minutes of his disjointed song. The one note off-key sound is rather like a referee's whistle. However, his bright plumage and whistles did animate an otherwise quiet taiga forest. At kilometer 330 stumps of small spruce trees cut by hand can be seen along the right-of-way. Hand clearing is usually employed on northern highways to avoid damage to the surface insulating vegetation and organic material, such as peat. If the permafrost is not insulated it will melt causing roads to slump, such as those we saw at kilometers 161 and 163. While building the rail-bed to Churchill a train and its 8 flat-bed cars were derailed. It fell onto the muskeg and permafrost. The workmen left the area to get help. When the crew returned they were absolutely amazed!

The metal was a good conducter of the sun's heat and the ice quickly melted and totally absorbed the whole train without a trace (17). Modern northern roads are constructed using the technique called End Dumping. The vehicles always stay

Black Bear photo by Heather Neville

on the gravel fill and back-up to dump their load at the leading edge. The gravel is piled to a depth which will prevent conduction of heat through the peat to the permafrost below.

At kilometer 367 we reached the famed Eagle Plains Hotel. The site was chosen because of a rocky outcrop and its construction would not be compromised by the permafrost. The hotel was very quiet because the Peel and Mackenzie River crossings were closed. The RV pads had half a meter of snow on them; so we stayed in the carpark and plugged into a nearby electrical outlet. Chris, Norm, Brandy, Diane and the rest of the staff were very friendly and we were quickly made to feel at home. Heather enjoyed a well-cooked hamburger steak and a veal cutlet for me. The photographs on the walls were hung by Dick North, commemorating the Lost Patrol. The bar was called the Millen Lounge after a man who died trying to apprehend the Mad Trapper. It too was decorated with appropriate photographs. It was still light at 11pm when we went to bed. A robin singing woke me at half past midnight! Dawn comes early at that time of year. At 1am a White-crowned Sparrow was vocalising and 1:30 was punctuated by a Fox Sparrow song. Musically dawn in the north had become an enlightening experience!

At kilometer 374 there is a bridge over the Eagle River. The river is a major feature meandering through the region. The valley is beautiful pristine wilderness with spruce and white birch all around. The Eagle drains into the Yukon via the Porcupine River. About 80 kilometers downstream from this crossing ended the 48 day chase for the Mad Trapper of Rat River and the largest manhunt by Mounties at that time.

The manhunt for the Mad Trapper of Rat River is one of the most infamous in Canadian history. It was all the more riveting because it took place in North America's last frontier. In the winter conditions of 1931-2, the Mounties used the remote community of Aklavik as a base to launch the manhunt for Albert Johnson. In addition to the extremely harsh conditions, and the resourcefulness of Johnson, several other factors added to the drama. Radios were becoming standard equipment in many North American homes and people could follow the chase in the form of a real life and death nightly serial! For example: two well-known northerners, Slim and Agnes Simmler lay in their tent every night on the Arctic coast and followed the drama on the wireless (23). One man defied a combined force of white trappers, First Nations people, and above all, the Mounties in a 48 day running battle. A legendary bush

TRAVELLING THE DEMPSTER

pilot named Wop May used his plane in what is believed to have been the first aerial pursuit in the Arctic (27). It was only a little over 3 years since the first plane had flown to Dawson! The trail was 240 km. long, north of the Arctic Circle and in temperatures of -40 degrees! Finally , Albert Johnson's history is still to this day a mystery, or is it (33)? The trail begins in 1926.

After seeing a posthumous picture of Albert Johnson, people in Dees Lake, northern British Columbia, recognised him as the man they knew as Arthur Nelson (32). Goldpan Creek was the site of a minor goldrush and Nelson arrived there in August, 1926. He built himself a cabin above Mosquito Creek using neither nail nor spike. It was still standing in 1972 and demonstrated Nelson's skill with an ax and a hand drill. Nelson seemed to have an inner hostility about him and some people recalled being uncomfortable around him. His eyes were like cold steel. He appeared to have a chilling indifference to the world. Art Nelson left abruptly after a year; told no one of his plans and left a bag of belongings hanging in a tree. The man who was often referred to as a loner started to trek north carrying a huge backpack. In July, 1931, he appeared at Fort McPherson going by the name of Albert Johnson. After purchasing supplies he headed for the Rat River. Johnson again built himself a cabin ominously near three other trap lines. A damper was placed on the Christmas celebrations at Arctic Red River when one trapper reported to Corporal Spike Millen that Johnson was springing his traps. Corporal King visited Johnson's cabin on December 28th, but the occupant not only failed to invite him in, but wouldn't even speak to him. King was concerned about this strange behaviour and decided to go to Aklavik to obtain a search warrant. At noon, on December 31st, 1931, King and three other men returned to the cabin. After calling, then knocking on the door, they were answered by a rifle shot and King was hit!

The injured Mountie was lashed to a sled and then started the historic dash to save King's life. The dogs were already tired. There were about 130 kilometers to travel. It soon became dark. 20 knot winds were blowing obliterating their back trail and the temperature was 40 below! They had to stop regularly to warm King's face against frostbite. Despite the poor conditions they reached Aklavik in 20 hours. The bullet had passed through the left and right chest without hitting any major organs. With the care of the doctor and nurses in the little hospital, and his own remarkable fitness, King was up and about in three weeks.

Inspector Eams had 11 men under his command. Aklavik also had access to the Royal Corps of Signals, which would prove invaluable. Eams lead a team of 9 men and 42 dogs to apprehend Johnson. He used the Signal Corps to ask Millen (at Arctic Red River) to meet him at the mouth of the Rat River. The posse left on January 4th and stopped briefly at Blakes Post to purchase 9 kilos of dynamite. Just before noon, on January 9th, Eams reached the cabin. There was smoke coming out of the chimney so he shouted for Johnson to come out. He added that King would live. Johnson, as on all other occasions, never said a word. The men were able to get close to the cabin but Johnson began a steady discharge of fire, which drove them back. Meanwhile, the temperature was minus 45 and Inspector Eams was aware of his diminishing supplies. Fires were lit to keep warm and Eams ordered the dynamite to be thawed out. Not a job for the squeamish! Kurt Lang volunteered to approach the cabin and throw explosives on the roof. The smoke stack and the roof were dislodged but Johnson kept firing.

At 3 in the morning of January 10th Eams threw his last 2 kilos of dynamite onto the cabin destroying most of it. To the surprise of all, Johnson was still shooting. One hour later Eams decided to return to Aklavik. Johnson had held them off for 15 hours! The

Signals Corps broadcast from radio UZK reporting that: "Johnson was still holding out." (21) At this time the epithet "Mad Trapper of Rat River" was used. On January 14th Millen revisited the cabin and found, not surprisingly, that Johnson had disappeared. Radio took on a greater importance and much of the public sympathy was with the courage of Johnson.

On January 16th a posse again set out, this time with a two-way radio. Meantime a snow storm had covered Johnson's trail. Millen's small party of four were getting weary. On January 28th they picked up a faint, two day old trail. Johnson was canny, crossing creeks on clear ice and following ridge tops where snow was hardpacked, leaving a poor trail. He often zigzagged in order to observe his backtrail. Johnson seemed to have tremendous energy and was travelling 2 km. to their 1, carrying his 100 kgm. backpack! He penetrated dense thickets of willow; climbed cliffs and still found time to snare squirrels. Then an Indian gave the posse a lead saying that he had heard a shot near the Bear River. On the trail they found discarded quarters of caribou meat, confirming the Indian's report. Finding a small fire down in a canyon they waited for Johnson. They could even hear him whistling as he moved in amongst spruce trees. But he never came out in the open. After dark, and in minus 50 degrees they retreated to camp. The trackers returned to the canyon and surounded Johnson's camp. One of the trackers slipped making enough noise to alert Johnson. He fired his 30-30 Savage rifle at Millen and ducked behind a log. In a harsh, cold atmosphere four tough Mounties faced an even tougher woodsman.

After waiting two hours Spike Millen decided to approach the fugitive. There followed an exchange of fire; Millen suddenly rose up and collapsed. He had been shot through the heart. Examining Johnson's camp the next day they found that he had cut steps in an ice-covered vertical cliff and escaped the canyon, still carrying his backpack. Millen's death was reported back to Aklavik on January 31st. Inspector Eams, when he got the news, realized that the media would have a field day. The Inspector had some grudging respect for the fugitive who could stay ahead of his trackers and dog teams.

It was at this point that Eams requested a plane. Not only could it help with tracking in daylight but it would drop supplies. Each dog ate 1 kgm. of fish per day. The request went up the line to the Minister of Justice before being approved. Wop May, an ace fighter pilot from the 1st World War actively joined the search on February 7th. He began ferrying supplies to Eam's party near the Barriere River. Other men were called in from as far away as Edmonton and Fort Norman to help with the hunt. The reputation of the Mounties was on the line and they all knew it (32).

Wop May could supply the trackers in less than 30 minutes from Aklavik; whereas the dog teams took 3 days. Meanwhile Johnson had travelled up the Barriere River. He was unable to light fires or use his rifle, lest he attract attention; so he used snares to catch small game. The soft snow made it necessary for him to expend great amounts of energy, breaking trail each day. On February 9th there was a blizzard and the fugitive chose this time to cross the ridges of the Richardson Mountains in his bid for freedom. In this barren alpine zone the windchill factor can reduce the temperature to minus 100! The Indians and trappers in the area all doubted that he could cross the mountains at that time of year. The Richardsons are the northern extension of the Rockies. So it was something of a surprise when Peter Alexy brought the news that Johnson's tracks had been seen to the west of the mountain peaks! On February 12th strange snowshoe tracks had been spotted east of Lapierre House. This physical feat was and is truly remarkable. Johnson headed first to the Bell then the Eagle Rivers in a southerly direction.

On February 13th Eams and some of his men were flown to Lapierre House and others attempted to cross Rat Pass. Johnson was able to use caribou tracks to disguise his own trail. On February 14th May spotted the tracks 32 km. up the Eagle from its confluence with the Bell. On the 15th fog kept May on the ground but Eams set out with one of the dog teams. The Eagle River meanders amongst low rolling hills and timber. The trackers left arrows on the ground, made with spruce branches, so that May could locate them when the weather improved. The men of Old Crow were preparing another posse in case Johnson tried to head down the Porcupine River. An old Shamman woman in the village cautioned them not to go, predicting he would be dead after one more sleep.

The sky was gradually clearing on the morning of the 17th when Eam's men took up the trail. They were on one of the hairpin turns of the river, the trackers having camped on one side of the pin and Johnson on the other. Johnson became confused when he ran across some old ski tracks. He turned back and ran straight into the posse at noon. The first Mountie to see him reported that Johnson was backtracking, thinking the posse was behind him. Hercy immediately started firing and other members of the posse joined in. Heading towards the river bank, Johnson whirled firing instantly. Hercy was lifted off the ground by the powerful bullet and cartwheeled into the snow. The slug smashed through his left elbow, plowed through his left knee then ripped through his chest. Albert Johnson wriggled out of his pack and used it for defence. The Mounties split up moving along each side of the river. Eams shouted twice to Johnson to surrender. The crossfire soon took its toll: one shot hit ammunition in Johnson's pocket causing it to explode. Other bullets hit him in the shoulder and side but he kept returning fire. A third time, Inspector Eams asked him to surrender: the only answer was the bark of his Savage rifle and a wave of his arm. The posse then poured bullets into Johnson's shallow refuge. Wop May had arrived and they were photographing the scene from above. They even heard the rifle sounds above the engine noise. After making a close pass, May could see that Johnson was dead. Sid May (no relation to the pilot) walked up at about that time and turned Johnson over. A bullet had passed through the Mad Trapper's spine leaving him face down, still holding the rifle in his right hand. Wop May said when he looked, Johnson was wearing the worst grimace of hate he had ever seen. Hercy was flown to Aklavik where he

Grave Marker Mad Trapper of Rat River

recovered and kept the slug that did all the damage. Johnson was buried in Aklavik and the grave marked with a tree stump, bearing the initials A J.

The Milepost (20) introduced me to a book called Trackdown (33), another book by Dick North. Albert Johnson was almost certainly, Johnny Johnson, a bank robber from North Dakota. Truth is sometimes stranger than fiction and Dick North is an amazing amateur sleuth.

Climbing out of the Eagle Valley we stopped at a 1 acre pond on the right. To my pleasure, I was able to record Horned

TRAVELLING THE DEMPSTER

Grebe, Northern Shoveller and Wood Frogs. Our GPS read N 66' and I wondered if these were the world's most northerly frogs. Just beyond the pond I heard high pitched calls from two birds. At first, they sounded like sandpipers. Then, as I listened more carefully, they started to sound like birds of prey. These became my first recordings of Rough-legged Hawks! According to The Birds of the Yukon Territory (1): "Its thin, hoarse scream is a characteristic sound of the northern tundra." This pair appeared territorial at the edge of the trees, with a cliff to the west. They nest more commonly along the Arctic Coast with the world's greatest density on Herschel Island. A First Nation's myth tells of how the hawk brought fire to the people. Crow places pitch on hawk's beak and sends him out to bring back fire. Hawk returns with fire but looses his long beak in the process.

At kilometer 405 is a signpost marking the imaginary line of the Arctic Circle. This line circles the planet at 66 degrees, 33 minutes north marking the outer limit where the sun never sets on June 21st. Conversely, at the winter solstice the sun does not appear above the southern horizon. The further north one travels from this point, the more days with the midnight sun, or conversely, total darkness in mid winter. George Calef (12) states: "For example in Inuvik at 68 degrees north the sun never sets from May 25th to July 18th each summer, and never appears between December 7th and January 6th." Fortunately, during those darkest days of winter, there is a glow below the southern horizon producing enough light to see and work outside for a few hours. Some northern citizens think the winter darkness is harder to endure than the cold temperatures. We have met people who drive the Dempster simply to reach this mysterious

JOHN NEVILLE

spot on the planet. This ridge above the tundra is certainly a good place to contemplate the universe and our place in it.

CHAPTER 6

THE RICHARDSON MOUNTAINS:
KILOMETERS 410 TO 492.

Including: Long-tailed Jaeger, Porcupine herd of Barren Ground
Caribou, Rock River Valley,
and the Northern Wheatear

The Richardson Mountains are the northern extension of the Rockies named after Franklin's second in command, Sir John Richardson, who twice accompanied Franklin to this part of the Arctic. The top of this range forms the boundary between the Yukon and Northwest Territories. On this section of the highway we found typical arctic tundra. High winds and continuous permafrost combine to create stunted vegetation on rounded and rolling terrain. Exceptions were streamside willow and spruce. We passed three beautiful Long-tailed Jaeger which came in to land amongst grassy tussocks on the tundra. Jaeger means hunter in German; the European name for this predator is Long-tailed Skua. These aggressive gull-like birds are sometimes referred to as pirates. They rob nests and snatch food from the beaks of other birds. In the winter months, they are technically pelagic, spending their time out at sea off the South American coast.

Sheep Creek crosses under the highway at kilometer 433. The foothills near this stream are used by caribou in spring and fall. The northern Yukon is home to the Porcupine herd of Barren Ground Caribou, taking their name from the Porcupine River. In the springtime approximately 180,000 animals travel northwesterly across the coastal plains so that the cows can bear their young in the Alaskan foothills. After only a few hours the calves can run faster than a human and keep up with the herd! The Alaskan foothills are an important part of the calving ground, but unfortunately, this region is threatened by possible petroleum exploration. The lengthening days and melting snow in late March and early April trigger the urge to migrate. Their winter range is in the spruce filled valleys and wind swept ridges of the Ogilvie and Richardson Mountains and the Eagle Plains. They proceed in single file, the leading cows breaking trail for the followers. The migration crosses the Dempster at many points. Their two month migration over hundreds of kilometers is a wonder of navigation and endurance! George Erickson in True North (16), describes their perils: "Being swept sideways by fast water and dashed to pieces over rapids." The reddish-brown calves are born in late June while there is still snow on the arctic tundra. The melting snow, misting over with fog, is not suitable for wolf dens and is therefore reasonably safe for the young caribou. Caribou milk is the richest of all mammals. After two weeks of nursing, the calves are able to graze independently on the blooming tundra flowers. The animals gradually form into larger and larger herds often numbering in the tens of thousands, as they feed across the Alaskan coastal plains. This is one of the world's greatest natural spectacles. I gained some appreciation for the size of the herds last November from a CBC news broadcast. The announcer described the main road in Labrador being blocked for three days by a migrating herd of caribou.

In the fall the Porcupine Caribou slowly move eastward on the return migration, skirting to the north of Old Crow flats and back into the Richardsons. The bulls lead carrying life-sustaining backpacks of fat weighing 14 kilos or more. The men of Old Crow hunt the fat caribou when they cross the Porcupine River. The caribou is a mainstay of Gwitchen life. Wolf, bear, nosebot fly and warblefly also prey on the caribou. The warblefly chooses the thin lightly furred skin on the belly or inner legs to lay eggs (29). After hatching, the saw-toothed larvae burrow into the animal's hide. They then migrate through the body to the warmth of a well-insulated back and lay up in a fibrous sack. By spring they have become a grub about the size of a jellybean, and they exit through the skin often leaving infected holes. Falling to the ground the grubs pupate into warbleflies which then look for a caribou to start the cycle again. When skinning caribou in the summertime Inuit will pinch the skin to find warblefly grubs and eat them as hors d'oeuvres (29).

The nosebot fly enter through the nostrils and lay eggs in the pharyngeal muscous membrane of the host animal. There, the wriggling larvae restrict breathing of the caribou and make them easier prey for wolf and bear. In People of the Deer (29), Farley Mowat described removing 130 of these giant maggots, about an inch long, from the nose and throat of one doe. These parasitized animals only gain temporary relief when the mature larvae fall to the ground to pupate again.

If the main herds are going to winter near the Dempster they can usually be seen by early October. The rutting bulls sometimes display alongside the highway in the southern Ogilvies. The successful bulls mate with a number of females. The animals have large hooves to traverse the snow, and fur around the muzzle to protect them when

JOHN NEVILLE

foraging for lichen under the snow. One comforting note: their coats are comprised of hollowed hairs which provide excellent insulation. The nostrils are valved to restrict the passage of cold air, snow and insects when grazing. They spend up to 12 hours a day pawing aside the snow to reach lichens, sedges, horsetails and other low growing plants. The sense of smell is the primary means of locating the 5 kilos of food needed each winter day. Eating, resting and staying alert for predators is the lot of a caribou.

A subspecies of caribou maintain a small foot note in the long list of animal extinctions. The Dwarf Caribou lived on Haida Gwaii. In 1878, George Dawson (as in Dawson City and Dawson Creek) wrote of the possibility of elk on northern Graham Island. He later changed the name to caribou. The animal was eventually known as Dawson's Dwarf Caribou. As with the Ivory-billed Woodpecker, the scientific world demanded specimens, which meant dead caribou. One such specimen found its way to the Victoria museum and was examined by the naturalist Ernest Thompson Seton in 1900. Seton declared it to be a new species, but his conclusions were not accepted. David Day, in his book Noah's Choice (15), describes the contraversy in detail. To foreshorten this sad episode, hunters found and shot 2 bulls, a cow and one calf in 1908, instantly proving their existence and extinction at one and the same time.

We pulled into Rock River Campground at kilometer 448. While we were having supper a raptor started calling very close by. I quickly gathered together my equipment and from just behind the Bird Mobile pressed the record button. The bird was high in some spruce trees. The surrounding area is open tundra but this protected river valley has trees 10 to 15 m. tall. After recording the bird Heather and I went out to search for the raptor: Osprey and Goshawk being at the top of my suspect list. We didn't find him so got out song guides and our books. The Northern Goshawk matched my recording and Birds of the Yukon Territory listed Rock River as one of the sitings for this bird. It was a little windy (geophony) but it was definitely a recording I could use. To add to our pleasure, it was a species we had not even considered as possible for this trip! The Rock River valley is known as an important hunting ground for Gwitchen people. The archeological records indicate their presence for about 8,000 years. Fences were built up to a kilometer long funneling the animals into traps and snares. The people could then dispatch the caribou with arrows and spears.

On May 22nd, we drove a few kilometers out of the Rock River valley onto the tundra before stopping for breakfast. It was quite windy so recording was not practical. With the wide vistas of tundra, mountains and valley below Heather produced sausage, eggs and toast, followed by hot buttered raison scones and the remains of the coffee. Not bad for camping, eh! We took a walk up the road and out onto the tundra before moving on. Falco ran, leaped and circled us expressing the pleasure of his freedom. The wind did not stop us hearing White-crowned Sparrow, Wilson's Snipe and Golden Plover. The tussocks were a little raised with lichen filling the spaces making walking awkward. The surface gravel below the lichen was wet where the permafrost was melting. Nearby snipe were copulating and giving their "chippa chippa" calls. The male spread his pointed wings to keep his balance while mounting.

The road ascended the mountains in easy stages. At kilometer 465 we reached a little pulloff at the boundary with the Northwest Territories. The elevation was 961 m. This was the third time we crossed a continental divide, where water flows west to the Pacific and east to the Arctic. The mountain range was raised up about

JOHN NEVILLE

100 million years ago from an ancient sea. It comprises limestone and coral from the sea bed. The political boundary also represents the eastern edge of Beringia and on the eastern slopes the western edge of the old Laurentide Glacier. The ice was hundreds of meters thick and its limits can be seen in the U-shaped valley we entered beyond this boundary. We followed instructions and turned our watches forward one hour to Mountain time. Neither of us was clockwatching but it is good to be in the right zone.

Shortly afterwards, in a rocky ravine, Heather noticed a pretty

Sunrise on the Richardsons by Heather Neville

songster out of the window. He turned out to be a Dempster special, the Northern Wheatear. It flew across the ravine several times allow-ing me to record the "distinctive flight song, a jumble of liq-uid and grating notes as the bird flaps and planes like an outsize black and white butterfly" (18). It seemed to favour the rocky talus and the sluffing surface called solifluction. This small critter is known as a Wheatear in Western Europe and a Northern Wheatear on our continent. It winters in north Africa and southeast Asia and some of them fly north through Asia across the Bering Strait to nest in the rugged mountains of the Yukon, NWT and Alaska. About 20 kilometers further on, I got the chance to record another specialty bird, the Long-tailed Jaeger. This time they flew above me with long pointed wings and a black cap, call-ing as they went. Both recordings might have been longer but I was very pleased with what I had.

The route down the east side was much steeper. Bridges took the road over two deep gorges and into another valley. There was only just room for the road and a river. These rugged rock slopes would be a physical challenge in the summer to a well-equipped climber. It is all the more incredible to imagine how Albert Johnson and his pursuers traversed these frozen mountains in January.

CHAPTER 7

THE PEEL PLATEAU:
KILOMETERS 492 TO 541

*Including: Tundra, Lemming, Bird Mobile, Midway Lake and
high water on the Peel River*

Descending from the Richardsons we emerged onto a vast open lowland vista. At kilometer 495, with tundra in all directions the GPS read North 67 ' 10 " and West 135' 41", altitude was 564 m. "The Peel Plateau is a broad upland which sweeps downwards to the Peel River, offering a view of the relatively flat lands that stretch away for hundreds of miles towards Hudson Bay." (12) This is the 6th Region of the Dempster Highway (18). The Laurentide Glacier once covered this whole area. It was only prevented from moving further west by the height of the Richardson Mountains. The flora varies from hummock, tussock to stunted forests of spruce and tamarack, covered with many lakes and ponds. The reddish tinge of alder bark was noticeable amongst the bare deciduous trees.

Buds were appearing but leaves were still a couple of weeks away. By the end of May we were enjoying warm sunshine up until 10 or 11 at night. The early mornings were still quite cool, causing me to dress up warmly to go out recording. At the time, I did not fully appreciate the benefit of the cool mornings. By the third week in June, the temperature increases around the clock allowing insects to grow in profusion! The cooling temperatures in the fall transform this region into an ocean of golden-yellow, rich red and green colours.

The tundra is the barren plains between the coast and the Boreal Forest to the south. Tundra is also found on arctic islands and very similar landscapes exist on mountain tops called Alpine Tundra. These frozen grasslands change suddenly into a frenzy of living activity under the midnight sun. The permafrost is permanently frozen water, soil and rocks reaching down a hundred meters or more. In the short summer, the surface permafrost melts creating shallow ponds and muskeg. Water cannot drain through the frozen land and roots cannot penetrate it; therefore, together with a short but intense growing season, all vegetation remains low and stunted. The Arctic wildflowers have adapted to the short summer, and grow, bloom and seed in the long summer days. Another interesting feature is the low rainfall on the tundra, which can be likened to a desert in many ways. The long winters prevent organic material breaking down, although bacteria and fungi are present. Lichen are a form of plant comprising bacteria and fungi working together in a symbiotic relationship. In sheltered areas, like the Peel and Mackenzie river valleys, trees and shrubs do grow, but not as tall as in the forest further south. On well-drained soil, dwarf willow and birch grow with low growing grasses and herbs. Where bogs form sedges, rushes and lovely soft mosses can be found. A thin carpet of winter snow helps to insulate mosses and herbs. In the growing season the melting snow provides a modest water supply. The long summer days help the plants to convert the sun's rays into needed sugars. Because the arid arctic barrens receive about the same amount of moisture as the Mohave Desert the plants have evolved several moisture-conserving tricks. Constrained by low temperatures and a short growing season, Arctic plants fill every crevice that provides sufficient warmth, shelter and moisture. Poppies and Labrador Tea conserve heat and moisture with hairy stems. Others grow in tight insulating clusters. George Erickson (16) described the overall appearance: "The Tundra unrolls, a blossom flecked sea of green."

The insect life is not so diverse as elsewhere in the world. The mosquitoes and flies make up for this with sheer numbers! The Porcupine Caribou move into the mountain foothills to escape the swarming mosquitoes. The marshes and ponds are suddenly alive with waterplants, crustaceans, insect and fish life. Mosquitoes are most numerous in July and therefore it is the most uncomfortable month for mammals, like ourselves. The water surface becomes crowded with ducks, geese, and around the edges thick with plovers and sandpipers. Because the days are longer, and the food is abundant, the young birds receive more food and grow more quickly than their southern cousins. All the sparrows, thrushes, warblers and swallows raise a brood in short order, before heading south for the winter. Western Sandpipers are usually recorded flying south as early as the middle of July. Many of the arctic breeding birds migrate long distances. The Arctic Tern is the greatest athlete flying about 30,000 km. to the Antarctic and back in one year. Perhaps the most stirring sight around Old Crow in September is the large flocks of Snow Geese assembling for their southerly migration. I have marvelled at flock after flock passing overhead in Grand Prairie around Thanksgiving and again in the Fraser Delta in November. The yelping sounds often carry long distances, alerting the listener before the blue or white morphs appear.

A few critters have adapted for long dark winters on the tundra. White-tailed Ptarmigan find snowbanks deep enough to bury themselves in long tunnels. Except for a few black speckles their feathers turn pure white for camouflage. If the birds remain still they may go undetected by a hunting fox. Ptarmigan also grow feathers around their toes for insulation and to use like snowshoes on soft snow. These birds survive by eating twigs and leaf buds from willows and other plants. The large Snowy Owl is delicately coloured black and white in summer but changes to a milk white plumage for the winter. Only its eyes glow like large yellow lamps. These owls can and do catch ptarmigan but rely primarily on lemming for their Christmas dinner. One owl pellet usually contains about 6 lemming remains.

The lemming is an endearing little rodent, toast brown or gold in colour. It is an absolutely essential part of the foodchain in a vast, harsh area of the world's surface. One female lemming can have 5 litters per year, each litter having between 8 to 10 offspring! Young males and females can breed when they are only 3 weeks old. These busy little herbivores dig tunnels in the snow to feed on roots, moss and grasses. Because these critters are so prolific they eat up all the food around them provoking their famous migrations. When thousands of them are on the move they whistle quietly to stay in contact. Just like caribou they pause when reaching obstacles like creeks but pressure from behind soon forces them forwards. They are good swimmers so often survive. They are very light and can float like puffballs. However, if it is a large lake or the sea they become food for Glaucous Gull, Common Raven, Jaeger, Short-eared Owl, other raptors and fish. The Canadian Arctic is home to the Brown, Collared and four other species of Lemming. Like ptarmigan and Snowshoe Hare, the lemming changes to a protective white winter coat. Collared lemming develop two large toes on their front feet in the winter to help dig through ice and snow.

Legend has it that lemming commit mass suicide by jumping off cliffs into the sea. This is, of course, quite untrue. In 1958, the

JOHN NEVILLE

Walt Disney Studios reinforced the suicide myth in the film "White Wilderness". This Oscar winning movie about animals in the Arctic depicts lemming appearing to jump and the narrator referring to a "boom and bust" cycle every few years. The viewer was told that these rodents are driven by a compulsion or unreasoning hysteria to commit suicide. It was about two decades later that the public learned that Disney had imported lemming and lured them over the edge to mimic the script.

University of British Columbia scientists have been studying the lemming on the tundra south of Cambridge Bay and their changing populations. The lemming is an important part of the foodchain and its cyclic decline also affects the Snowy Owl, Rough-legged Hawk, Sandhill Crane, Jaegers, Glaucous Gulls, Weasles, Arctic Ground Squirrel and Arctic Foxes. There is less predation of geese by foxes when there are sufficient number of lemming. The decline in lemming occurred so quickly in 1993 that Snowy owls moved south in the middle of their breeding season. Two of the current theories for the cylic decline of lemming are:

1. biological stress
2. toxic chemicals in the food they eat.

Clearly the reasons for population crashes are complex and it will be fascinating to wait for more answers.

We were fortunate to be more or less self-contained on the tundra. Our motorhome surrounds us with a fiberglass carapace like the shell of a crab or lobster powered by a V-ten cylinder Ford engine.

Behind the driver's seat is a table with two bench seats. We can carry six people in comfort and safety. Under the table is Falco's bed and most of the time Falco is in it. Next there is a propane fueled fridge and storage cupboards. On the opposite side is the outside door, followed by a sink, cooking stove, microwave and storage units. At the rear is a double bed and bathroom side by side. The propane allows us to have hot water and a heater! Over the driving cab is a second bed which I use to store my recorder and microphones on, and Heather her photographic equipment. On the outside are storage compartments for hoses, cables, chairs, boots etc. The whole vehicle is 6.5 m. long, 2.5 m. wide and 3.3 m. tall. It was built in the year 1999. We bought it this March with 81,000 km. on the clock. So far it has proved very reliable and comfortable. The propane is very efficient heating the coach and hotwater. The latter is a wonderful luxury when washing on a cold morning. The 30 liter water tank in particular limits us to about four nights and five days on the road before replacing water, gas and propane. The relatively long period of time we could spend on the road had an interesting effect. I almost stopped looking at my watch except out of curiosity early in the morning. We did not listen to the radio or read newspapers. The Stanley Cup had been over for four days when we heard about the final game. On our way south later we noticed election posters. At first we thought there must be an election in the Yukon, but gradually realised there was a federal election underway. Not hearing "the news" definitely reduced mental stresses and allowed us to relax into the rhythms of the natural world.

At km. 476 there was a red sign for "men at work" and a culvert was obviously being repaired. The NWT roadside signs are red compared with the Yukon green markers. After the territorial boundary, on top of the Richardsons, the kilometer signs revert to zero. For simplicity's sake I will add the two together. The next red sign alerted us that the road widens to double as an emergency landing strip.

JOHN NEVILLE

At kilometer 509 the Bird Mobile followed a side road leading to Midway Lake. The ice was receding from the shore and a few wigeon squeaked their greeting when we arrived. A curious scene surrounded us: along the shore a stage had been constructed, plus tent platforms, lean-tos, teepee poles and pit toilets. This is the beautiful setting for an annual summer festival sponsored by Fort McPherson. Oldtime fiddling introduced by the Scottish fur traders, northern style jigs and oldtime dancing take place in the midnight sun. The canvas tents are specially constructed in Fort McPherson to incorporate a stove for cooking and heat. The festival now includes country musicians like George Fox. Tonight, two pairs of snipe and the ghosts of a few musicians are the only other occupants of the beach, as we settle in for the night.

As the Peel Plateau slowly descends towards the river valley more and more flocks of ducks fly above us going in the same direction. We were travelling at 30 kph. when a large-headed hawk passed us by gliding and gently flapping his broad wings across the tundra. He suddenly dove and came up with a small mammal. A second Hawk Owl soon arrived to share breakfast on a nearby ridge. A Sandhill Crane walked out on the tundra and allowed us to watch him. I tried unsuccessfully to record him but instead got a really good recording of Blue-winged Teal.

At kilometer 530 we stopped at a magnificent overlook to the Peel River. It was too overcast for good photographs but the waterway was 3 or 4 km. across. The hamlet of Fort McPherson was just visible downstream to the left, on the opposite bank. We descended the steep grade to the river with Heather gearing right down and still needing to use the brakes sometimes. At the bottom we found the Peel in flood with large chunks of ice, and trees being carried along in the current. The sign at waters edge said kilometer 539, "Ice Bridge Closed". A local fisherman spoke to us from his cabin and explained that the river was about 6 m. higher than the ferry could handle. The ice had gone out 4 days ago and 4 of the fishing cabins had been washed away. Apparently a huge ice jam, 20 m. tall, had built up at the junction of the Peel and Mackenzie Rivers, backing up the water. Other cabins had their furniture piled up on rooves. It was May 23rd, our granddaughter's first birthday. We decided to turn around and do some leisurely birding.

CHAPTER 8

THE PEEL MACKENZIE LOWLANDS:
KILOMETER 541 TO 615

Including: An anxious ferry crossing, Fort McPherson,
The Gwitchen, the fabled Mackenzie River,
Richard Bonnycastle and Ruby Kasook.

Along the banks of the Peel and Mackenzie Rivers grow large stands of White Spruce, cottonwood and birch trees, but the majority of the lowlands comprise muskeg, stunted Black Spruce, with an understorey of shrubs and mosses. On the evening of June 1st we again arrived at the Peel River crossing. Men were stringing the ferry cables with an anticipated opening the next morning. It was a warm humid evening and for the first time the screen door needed closing to keep the insects out. We heard our first Arctic Loons which were just as thrilling as Common Loons. Their size was notably smaller but the sounds were just as wild and wonderful.

The GPS read N 67' 20", W 134' 52". The altitude was 31 m., the closest we had been to sea level since leaving the west coast. Just after 4 pm we drove onto the ferry , named after a Gwitchen elder, C. F. Abraham Francis. The gravel ramps were still under construction. When the Bird Mobile's front wheels were on the ferry ramp the hitch at the rear dug into the soft gravel bringing us to a halt. The boat ramp could not be lowered any more. So, a frontend loader was positioned behind the motorhome. A chain was attached to the bucket and looped under our towing bar. This allowed the Bird Mobile to be lifted off the ground and chalks to be placed under the rear wheels. We became quite nervous when the whole vehicle wobbled in space! Others onboard took photographs of our predicament. Our anxiety subsided as we slowly drove onboard to the cheers of the passengers. As we made the crossing the GPS registered the ferry moving along its cables at 4.5 kph.

At kilometer 550, we took the turning to Ft. McPherson, population 952. The local name is Tetlin Zheh. Ft. McPherson was named after Murdoch McPherson in 1848, chief trader of the Hudson's Bay Company. There were two stores and we chose the CO-OP which had all the provisions we needed, including the "large breed chunks" of dog biscuit that Falco enjoys. All the houses were built on stilts and the pipes to the recreation center and other public facilities were above ground for winter maintenance. The residents were very friendly and easily laughed when we got into conversation.

Arctic Loon

The local cafe owner had just locked up when we arrived but learning our intention quickly reopened and showed us the menu. A local teacher was still inside eating. He described his afternoon trapped in the school elevator due to a power failure.

The visitors' center had really good Gwitchen exibits showing the skilled workmanship that went into the construction of snow-shoes, fishing traps, canoes and river boats. For example, after travelling into the mountains for caribou and moose in the winter they returned by large moosehide boats. Each 9 m. boat needed 14 mooseskins sewn together with sinews and stretched around spruce frames. The seams were sealed with spruce gum. Perhaps as many as 50 families would travel downstream in the moosehide boats for the fishing along the lower Peel. The skins would then be re-cycled for other uses. Jean Aspin's Arctic Daughter (2) points out the difficulties of butchering a moose in the wilderness. To begin with, the animal is bigger than a horse! It took three days of hard work before trying to find room for all the meat in their canoe. "We finished cutting the last quarter into strips on the fourth day and began the process of breaking and boiling the long bones for their fat." The butchering site was also visited by grizzly, wolf, fox, raven and flies. Jean Aspin and her husband were determined not to waste their bounty just like the Gwitchen people.

Some of the traditions and stories of 300 years ago would have been passed on orally for thousands of years. The stories of giant beaver for example have been confirmed in the fossil records of North America and Northern Europe. Local people still move up and down the Peel to fish, trap and hunt in the traditional manner. A present day fishing camp was already functioning as we passed towards Ft. McPherson. Floats marked the position of nets out in the river.

Much of the Dempster Region has been occupied by Gwitchen people for many centuries. A display panel at the Arctic Circle pullout suggests 20,000 years, while at Rock River it's thought to be 8,000 years. The Gwitchen belong to the great family of

TRAVELLING THE DEMPSTER

Athabaskan-speaking people spread across the vast areas of the far north between Alaska and Hudson Bay. The Athabaskans are divided into 25 linguistic groups, including the Chipewyan, Slave and Hare people. Before modern times the Gwitchen were believed to have numbered about 1,500, split amongst 6 groups, occupying most of the upper drainages of the Porcupine, Peel, and Arctic Red Rivers.

These people are highly adapted to the harsh subarctic conditions (12) being skillful hunters of caribou and moose, and craftsmen of light snowshoes which allow them to run in the soft snow. The Gwitchen language has a close relationship to Hopi, Navaho and Apache. These hunter-gatherers took advantage of all the resources of a harsh homeland. In the fall, the Peel River people moved into the Richardson Mountains, up the Blackstone, Hart and Wind Rivers. Here they hunted caribou for their communal meat camps. Laura Burton (9)described them arriving in Dawson each December with their fast brightly decorated dogsleds. "They were a magnificent looking people with long black hair, great sleekness, high foreheads, good noses, strong white teeth and a straight look in their eyes." They employed traps with long wing fences to direct the animals into a corral or pound for harvesting. This technique was also employed by plains people (with piles of rocks) to direct buffalo to the edge of cliffs. The fences were constructed of spruce, joined with roots. The animals could then be snared or dispatched with arrows and spears. If the caribou failed to show up in sufficient numbers the hunters would look for moose and sheep. They stayed in the mountains all winter and only moved down to the Peel for fishing, in the spring. Here they spent the summer fishing and trading with neighbouring people as some of them do to this day.

Government regulations in the 1950's caused permanent settlements to grow in order that Gwitchen children could attend school. The Gwitchen language and culture are now taught again in the schools. Because Inuit and Gwitchen lived in small family groups suitable partners were scarce. This sometimes brought about raiding parties to obtain wives. With the coming of European traders, interaction between Inuit, Gwitchen and Chipewyan quickly increased. Today these three groups, plus people of European descent, live in harmony in all the communities from Hay River to Inuvik. When the first Hudson's Bay opened a trading post at Ft. McPherson, Gwitchen came rarely. Hunting remained their most important occupation. By the 1880's most Gwitchen had dog teams and traps for martin and other fur bearing animals. The furs were traded for tobacco, beads, tea and firearms. Some of the miners employed Gwitchen as guides during the Goldrush and the people learned about trading for money. Many of the Gwitchen moved to Dawson City by 1901 and were employed by the miners, NWMP and woodcutting for the paddlewheelers. It was not until 1910 that the people started to return to Ft. McPherson. Today the Dempster Highway has provided economic and small business opportunities for the people.

Our next stop was a turnoff near Frog Creek. An old gravel pit with two interconnecting ponds provided a lovely setting for our camp. Spotted Sandpipers called, hopped and bobbed around the shoreline. Their "wheat wheat" calls were echoes of the sounds we had heard around many other Canadian lakes. The sun allowed us to sit out until 10 pm and there were no bugs. Wigeon, scaup and scoter also shared this quiet haven with us. The next morning, June 4th , we headed towards the Mackenzie ferry. A Trumpeter Swan bugled a last farewell. The beige coloured road led us towards the "Great River". We passed large blue lakes, dark green spruce and light green tamaracks. The road suddenly dipped down to the river. The valley was lined with cliffs and the Arctic Red River flowed in from our right. The community of Arctic Red River was on a hillside also to the right.

The ferry, Louis Cardinal, had difficulty manoeuvring against the strong current to reach us. A small gravel bar had been constructed for protection on the upstream side. We had heard that not enough paint had been ordered for the boat and sure enough only the front half had been painted. When the current took us quickly downstream the ferry was travelling at 11.7 kph. Sharing the ride was a campervan and a young RCMP officer and his family making a transfer.

The Mackenzie is one of the world's greatest river systems. It ranks 12th for drainage area, and 11th for total discharge. With headwaters covering the Finlay in British Columbia, the Athabaska in Alberta's Southern Rockies and the Lockhart on the barren lands of the Northwest Territories, it drains an area larger than any other Canadian river: 1,094,324 square km. It is Canada's only navigable river to the Arctic. This waterway provided a trading corridor for the Hudson's Bay Company. Before the Dempster Highway was completed in 1979 barges on the Mackenzie provided the only bulk transportation to Inuvik and Aklavik. Since the river was only open from June to September pressure for a road grew with oil exploration in the Beaufort Sea.

In A Gentleman Adventurer (5) Heather Robertson uses Dick Bonnycastle's diaries to describe life around trading posts on the Mackenzie and along the Arctic Coast. In the 1920's the Hudson's Bay paddlewheeler "Distributor" used to call at Arctic Red River for furs and supplies. Before taking up his post in the Arctic, Dick Bonnycastle was obviously enjoying life aboard. The Captain mixed "excellent cocktails made from alcohol, old Buck rum, milk, eggs, vanilla and sugar. He is a splendid bartender and I must get his recipes." Returning to Arctic Red River in late September,

JOHN NEVILLE

Bonnycastle was taking his accounting job very seriously: "Staff and organisation in this district are both, I'm afraid, very weak." He left on October 8th in a little boat called The Bluefish before the Mackenzie froze up for the winter. Richard Bonnycastle later became well known as the first Chancellor of Winnipeg University and the creator of Harlequin Books.

Round about the time Dick Bonnycastle was exploring the Mackenzie another very different young person, Ruby Kasook, was also coming to maturity along the river. I'll let Bill Hill (23) tell the story about his mother-in-law : "Margo's mother was born in the early part of the century just north of the Yukon mainland on Herschel Island. Both of her parents died during the Spanish flu epidemic, 1918, that swept the world, leaving something like 50 million dead (and we worry about Sars, West Nile and Avian flu!). Still a baby, she moved in with relatives, somewhere on the Mackenzie Delta. Ruby was showing signs of the flu and they thought it may have been TB so they shipped her south to the hospital at Hay River. The disease she had contracted was pulmonary pneumonia. The signs were almost identical to TB, but of course in those days they didn't have the means to do blood analysis in the north. The long and the short of this was that they kept her down south for 6 years incarcerated in a residential school! The whole concept of residential schools was an afront to humanity, and a point of shame for the Canadian government. I could say a whole lot about this system, and the harm it did to the indigenous culture but I think I will refrain. That it was done in the name of Christianity was perhaps its most shameful aspect. Ruby (Margo's mum) didn't really have much memory of this time other than life was hard and you had to work, work, work. Not a very pleasant way to be brought up. The part that Ruby related to me, which really caught my attention was the trip back north. What an adventure she had: Part of it was just being away from Hay River, and all the evil associated with it. But generally it was the smell of freedom, and returning to the land of her ancestors. This was in the early thirties, and travel on the Mackenzie River was still done by sternwheeler. Ruby, a young woman by now, was enchanted by all that she saw: the people, the vistas, the huge amount of wood the boilers used up and stopping every 33 km. to pick up fresh supplies. The very first time she heard a musical instrument was on this trip. One of the crew members had a concertina, and when she heard it she was so astonished she fell down. Being able to speak in her own language was welcome, and being treated kindly for the first time in many years was so very nice, but the biggest surprise was the crew of the sternwheeler. They had this habit you see of pissing over the side whenever the urge took them, and Ruby told me with a twinkle in her eye: 'the very first time I saw a man's penis!' She went on to mother 18 children, no small feat. I can only say that her life was a productive one."

CHAPTER 9

THE EXPLORERS

Includes: Mackenzie and Franklin Expeditions

First Nations people have used the Mackenzie river as a transportation corridor for thousands of years. Unfortunately, most of their knowledge and experience is lost to us. The written record of Europeans reaches back little more than two centuries. A member of the Northwest Trading Company, Alexander Mackenzie, left Fort Chipewyan on June 3rd, 1789. With a small company of Indians and voyageurs he crossed Lake Athabaska heading north to find a trading route across North America to the west coast. The Rapids of the Drowned at Fort Smith caused him to portage for the only time on his historic voyage. The White Pelican colony on the islands above the rapids were noted and are still there today. He continued down the Slave River, across 480 km. of Great Slave Lake and down the Great River which now bears his name. The native words for Great River are "Deh Cho". When it became clear that the river was heading north, Mackenzie called it Disappointment River to match his feelings! They reached the Arctic Ocean on July 14th, 1789, the same day the French Revolution officially began. It was a tremendous discovery for Europeans, but not the ocean Mackenzie was seeking.

In 1792 he tried again, this time heading west up the Peace River from Lake Athabaska. His journey took him across the Rockies, down part of the not yet named Fraser River and westwards to

TRAVELLING THE DEMPSTER

Bella Coola. We travelled Highway 20 from Williams Lake to Bella Coola last year. The route is still challenging 200 years later. The road descends a 600 m. cliff known locally as "The Hill". The dropoff is not for the faint hearted! On the ferry to Port Hardy we passed the rock where Mackenzie recorded his arrival on July 22nd, 1793. His original script is long gone but the words are now carved into the rock and filled with white concrete for better visibility. "Alex Mackenzie from Canada by land 22nd July 1793". The Mackenzie party retreated quickly from the coast encouraged by hostile Indians. Captain George Vancouver was also on the coast that summer, for his second season, only missing Mackenzie at Bella Coola by six weeks! If Mackenzie had had the desire he could have gone southwest from Lake Athabaska, up the Athabaska River. That route would have taken him to the Rockies and via the Punch Bowl to the Columbia River. It would have been an easier route and one which David Thompson and many fur traders used just a few years later. When Sir Alexander Mackenzie's journal Voyages from Montreal (26) was published, President Thomas Jefferson obtained a copy. The President became most anxious to establish an American presence in the Oregon Country. The Lewis and Clarke Expedition set out in 1804 and reached the mouth of the Columbia in 1805. In June 2002, we had enjoyed a visit to Wood Buffalo National Park where Mackenzie had started his two historic journeys. Later, a ferry took us across the outlet of Great Slave Lake which is also the beginning of the Mackenzie River at Fort Providence. That particular June morning a thin cover of ice chips were egressing Great Slave Lake and pushing the ferry sideways. At all these sites we had been impressed by the size and power of the river and the boldness of the early explorers. After his travels Mackenzie settled in his Scottish homeland, purchased a substantial share of the Northwest Company, and enjoyed his title until his death in 1820.

Before leaving England in 1819 Franklin consulted with Sir Alexander Mackenzie. At age 14, John Franklin joined the Royal Navy and had an eventful career. During the Napoleonic Wars he participated in the Battles of Copenhagen and Trafalgar. In the American War, he took part in the attack on New Orleans. Later, he was shipwrecked on an Australian reef. At the end of the Napoleonic Wars many Royal Naval personnel were paid off; however, Franklin's career continued. He commanded his own ship, the Trent, into the Arctic in 1818 and got his first experience of arctic pack ice.

In 1819, Franklin was ordered by Earl Bathurst, the Colonial Secretary, to make his first overland trip to the Arctic. At that time there was minimal knowledge of Canada's Arctic coast and therefore of a possible Northwest Passage. In 1771, Samuel Hearn reached the mouth of the Coppermine River and eighteen years later came Mackenzie's famous exploration. These were the only known points of reference along the north coast. In addition to charting, Franklin was to study geomagnetism for navigation, Aurora Borealis, weather conditions, Inuit behaviour and details of natural history. Doctor, later Sir John Richardson, was the surgeon and responsible for the study of natural history. Midshipmen Hood and Back were members of the party and later had important rivers named after them. Franklin consulted with the Hudson's Bay Company and members of the Northwest Trading Company before leaving England. Unfortunately, the conflict between the two trading companies was then at its apex and very nearly wrecked the expedition. The party travelled by canoe from Hudson Bay to Fort Chipewyan. On September 13th, 1819, Franklin described; "The light yellow of the fading poplars formed a fine contrast to the dark evergreen of the spruce." Along the waterways, he mentioned willows of an intermediate hue, bright purple tints of Dogwood, brown shades of Dwarf Birch and gay yellow flowers of the Shrubby Cinquefoil. The boreal forest looks much the same today. He also commented on the noisy Gray Jay. He referred to them as "Whisky Johnnie" after the Chipewyan name "Wiska Chan". Like Peter Pond and Sir Alexander Mackenzie, they left the Churchill River system via the 20 km. Messia portage to the Athabaska waterway.

On July 18th, 1820, Franklin left Fort Chipewyan, paddled by voyageurs. Indian guides and hunters were added to the group at Fort Providence. The Indians chose a place on the Winter River for their quarters and called it Fort Enterprise. After a short exploration to the north and east to the Coppermine River they settled into a log house for the winter. It was here that the shortage of supplies first became apparent. This caused George Back to make a 1,750 km. roundtrip to Fort Chipewyan on snowshoes, November till March, returning with some provisions. The two midshipmen had come close to a duel over a pretty Indian girl called Green Stockings. Was their conflict the reason Back was sent to Fort Chipewyan? They headed out again in June, 1821, for the Coppermine River but sadly still undersupplied. Two birchbark canoes were taken, together with the gum and pitch from spruce trees for repairs. At the mouth of the Coppermine, Samuel Hearn was honoured by naming a promontory Cape Hearn. Using the two canoes, they travelled east along the coast. A lucky opportunity occurred when a cash of Inuit supplies was found on an island. Having taken some seal skins to repair their shoes, they left a copper kettle, awls and beads in exchange. It's hard to imagine this party travelling an unknown rocky coast with icebergs to seaward and changing weather in frail birchbark canoes. They were able to chart the coast for 550 km. with latitude and longitude references and named many features, including Bathurst Inlet, after the Colonial Secretary. In August, gales and diminishing supplies of pemican forced them to turn back. At W 110'5" on August 22nd they named a last feature "Point Turn Again".

A terrible struggle now began as they returned up the Hood River and across the barren treeless landscape. Food became very scarce causing them to eat berries, lichen and leather clothing. Franklin came close to drowning in one river and lost a precious journal. Even George Back, the strongest member of the naval party (who later became an admiral), was driven backwards by the wind and used a stick for support. Franklin records that on October 6th the whole party ate their old moccasins before trudging on in the snow. Richardson and Hepburn stayed back with the weakest members of the party, including Hood. When Franklin and others finally reached Fort Enterprise they were very distressed to find no supplies waiting for them. "The whole party wept, not so much for our own fate, as for our friends in the rear whose lives depended entirely on our sending immediately relief from this place." When Richardson arrived at Fort Enterprise on October 29th, 1821, he had to report that Hood and Michell were dead. He further surmised in his report that Hood had been murdered by Michell and hinted at cannibalism to sustain life. The party was close to total starvation when rescued at Fort Enterprise by some Indians who eventually helped them to Fort Providence.

The party had come very close to a total disaster, however, in retrospect they were able to map and name about 500 km. of the Arctic coast east of the Coppermine River. No mean feat. They discovered that traditional canoes were unsuitable for saltwater travel. The weather conditions, modes of transportation, the culture of First Nations people and how to obtain food in the Arctic were all new problems for British Naval personnel. Franklin had overcome

TRAVELLING THE DEMPSTER

some great obstacles, and greatly increased British knowledge of the polar sea. With so much hardship and discomfort it's hard to imagine anyone wishing to return to the Arctic!

However, Franklin made a proposal to the British government and his plans were accepted in January, 1825, for a second expedition. It is a credit to Franklin that Richardson and Back requested to travel with him again! The fur companies had amalgamated in 1821 under the name of the Hudson's Bay Company. Franklin again asked for assistance from the governor and the company factors in Canada. The company no longer had fueding distractions and was able to respond positively to the request. Governor George Simpson had serious doubts about Franklin: "The commander was incompetent and ill prepared" (35) probably referring to his first expedition.

A century later, in the Friendly Arctic (37), Stephanson lamented how long it took the British to adopt the ways of the Inuit. This time food and support were supplied as necessary. The traders advised him that Great Bear Lake would be the best place to winter, as fish could be caught and it was reasonably near the mouth of the Mackenzie River. With hindsight, Franklin knew that birchbark canoes were too frail for large waves and ice, so had special boats built in England. They were made of mahogany and ash, pointed at each end and could carry two to three tons of cargo. The largest was 26 ft. and the other two boats were 24 ft. in length. Another innovation was a light craft covered in waterproof material, weighing about 40 kgm. for crossing rivers. Mr. Macintosh of Glasgow (famous for his waterproof coats) provided the boat cover and waterproof suits for the travellers. This time, the supplies included chocolate, ample ammunition, tobacco, paper for preserving specimens, and many other practical items for Europeans.

The expedition set out in the spring of 1825 for a two year trip. A sad message reached them enroute. Franklin heard that his wife had died of tuberculosis leaving their daughter Eleanor to be looked after by one of his sisters. When they reached Fort Resolution, on the shore of Great Slave Lake, the voyageurs danced all night to the bagpipes, despite having paddled for 36 of the last 39 hours! The fur trade had developed the voyageur into a truly super human being! Franklin and some of the party proceeded to the mouth of the Mackenzie while others stopped at Great Bear Lake. Franklin landed on Garry Island, named Whale Island by Mackenzie. Many seal and whales were seen sporting on the waves. Gifts were left for the Inuit before they returned to Great Bear Lake on September 5th, 1825. The party now numbered 50, including 2 Inuit interpreters, 5 Chipewyan hunters, women and children. The log house was nearly complete and named Fort Franklin after their commander. Two additional buildings were constructed to aid fishing. In 1958, Peter Corley-Smith visited the site of one of the buildings (known as Fort Confidence) where the foundations and chimney were still standing. "The whole building had been about the size of a two car garage, but all cabins built by whitemen in those days were called forts." (14)

In the fall the nets yielded 3 to 5 hundred fish daily. During the winter months the men learned to read and write. In November Franklin wrote about "the amusements of skating" and historians still argue that this is the earliest reference to ice hockey (35). Numbers increased to 60 souls at Christmas, including representatives of 4 or 5 First Nations, and songs were sung in English, Gaelic and French. The winter appears to have passed in reasonable comfort with a moose having been shot in February to augment the diminishing fish supply. On May 16, 1826, Franklin reported the return of swallows, geese and swans. We noted Violet-green Swallows at the beginning of the Dempster Highway, May 11th but the swans had preceded us.

On July 3rd, Franklin gave Doctor Richardson his instructions. He was to explore and chart the coastline from the Mackenzie eastwards to the estuary of the Coppermine River, then return overland to Great Bear Lake, thus linking the known coastline from the previous expedition. At Point Separation "the evening was spent in the most cordial and cheerful manner" (35) before the two parties separated. By 6 am on July 4th the boats were fully packed and ready to go. Franklin and Back could not help comparing their well-equipped boats with the previous disastrous trip! They headed northwest with three months of supplies to explore westward from the estuary. Lieutenant George Back was in charge of the 2nd boat named Reliance. Franklin's boat was called the Lion. Pulling into an island they attempted to make friends with the Inuit. The scene became ugly with the Inuit attempting to carry off the boat's supplies. Franklin called the place Point Pillage! The party's Inuit interpreter, Augustus, managed to persuade his kinfolk to return most of the stolen items. On July 17th, a lead in the ice allowed them to approach Herschel Island and meet a friendlier group of Inuit. The boats travelled more than 40 km. on August 3rd and Franklin referred to the nearby mountains as the British Mountains which is part of what we call Beringia. By August 6th Franklin noted that "the nights were drawing in, and the mens' legs were sore and swollen from dragging the boats through mud and cold water." Longitude was determined to be W 149'37 " and latitude N 70'24". They left Return Reef on August 18th and started their journey back to Fort Franklin. At Foggy Island there was enough driftwood to build a warming fire. At another stopover Inuit women sowed sealskin soles onto the men's moccasins to make them more durable. The same Inuit warned of a possible ambush by mountain Indians at the mouth of the Mackenzie. They reached Fort Franklin safely on September 21st. Richardson had returned on September 1st. In a report to the British government Franklin described 1,000 km. of newly discovered coastline to the west.

Richardson in his explorations noted Bank's Swallows living along the riverbank. He admired the Inuit, translated parts of their language and purchased some of their weapons. On 13th July they visited Atkinson Island and described 13 Inuit huts and a large assembly hall. Richardson recognised Dwarf Willow, Thrift and eight other plants he knew from Scotland. On July 18th the scent of a beautiful Flox and a handsome cruisiform plant were noted. The latitude at Cape Bathurst was N 70' 36", the most northerly point for the whole expedition. An extensive bay was named in honour of Franklin. Captain Parry, Viscount Melvil and others were also distinguished by having geographical features named after them. Dolphin and Union Strait were named after their very dependable boats. This strait was occasionally traversed later by sailing ships such as HMS Enterprise in 1852 and 1853. However, it was not until the advent of nuclear submarines and polar icebreakers that the area has been traversed easily. The two boats were deposited at Bloody Fall (where Hearne had witnessed a massacre) and the trek upstream and across country began. Richardson praised his crew for their cheerful and obliging conduct. They had travelled about 3,000 km. on the round trip to Fort Franklin. The second in command, Kendle, was promoted to Lieutenant for his great service. Their part of the expedition had charted about 800 unknown km. of the north coast linking up with the chart of the first expedition. Richardson was an energetic man who left Fort Franklin in September 1826, before his commander had returned. He headed south to circumnavigate Great Slave Lake, in order to study its geography, geology, flora and fauna. On 18th June 1827,

Franklin and Richardson were reunited at Cumberland House. These two men had successfully charted more than 2,000 km. of Arctic coastline. Franklin was knighted in April, 1829, received a gold medal from the French Geographical Society and a honourary doctorate from Oxford University. One of Franklin's souvenirs was an Indian doll for his daughter Eleanor which now resides in the museum at Greenwich. Richardson published his monumental Flora Borealai Americana 1829 -1837 (35). George Back, having risen to the rank of captain, returned to the Arctic and explored the Back River in 1835.

Franklin went missing on his fourth and final visit to the Arctic. A message found in a cairn on King William Island announced that Franklin died on June 11th, 1847, attempting to sail through the Northwest Passage. Doctor John Richardson was to visit the Arctic once more with Doctor John Ray in search of his old friend and commander, Franklin, in 1848. It was Ray who first heard of the fate of Franklin's last expedition. Perhaps the romantic image of the grief- stricken, yet hopeful, Lady Franklin (his second wife) is a good place to end the saga. She climbed a slippery rock at the extreme north of Britain called Out Stack to pray for her husband's safe return. One of the nicest honours, in my opinion, bestowed on Franklin was the naming of Franklin's Gull which can still be seen flying all over the western Boreal Forest.

CHAPTER 10

THE MACKENZIE RIVER LOWLANDS TO INUVIK:
KM 615 TO 734

Including: Inuvik, Friendly People and Reindeer in the Delta.

The ferry was expertly maneuvered into position. The first truck off sank to its axles in the soft gravel before a cat pulled it out, with our full sympathy and understanding. A gravel bar had been built out on the upstream side to protect the landing. The ferry pulled back a few meters while some more work was done on the landing. Then it was our turn. After putting some extra planks in place, we cautiously moved forward! The planks moved the first time and we backed up. On the second attempt, Heather drove straight off and with the urging of the highway crew we kept going!

The road quickly left the willow bank, ascending to the plateau above. We let out a collective sigh of relief! The same friendly foreman who had supervised vehicles onto the Peel ferry had been in charge at this last tricky exit. We are still in the Peel Mackenzie Lowlands, but as Frisch puts it: "Taiga is thinner, swampier and shrubbier" (18). He also tells us that we can anticipate some dryer ground closer to Inuvik. The trees along our straight route were leaning in odd angles. The permafrost had created the "drunken forest", I had so often read about.

TRAVELLING THE DEMPSTER

Before we left Eagle Plains, I phoned Commercial Electronics in Vancouver with an urgent request for a replacement minidisc recorder. Mine would no longer function on batteries alone which made recording outdoors impossible. We decided to drive straight through to Inuvik and reach the Post Office, if possible, before closing time. The gravel highway changed to smooth pavement about 10 km out of town and all the little rattles in the Bird Mobile stopped. Inuvik is the administrative center for the Mackenzie Delta. The name means, "the place of men", in the local Inuit language. The community was built in 1954 to replace Aklavik, "the place of the Brown Bear", which floods each spring during breakup.

Inuvik is a modern community with a large hospital and airport for the Western Arctic. The blocks of townhouses are built on stilts like Fort McPherson. We had arrived in a town of 3,500 on the east channel of the river, surrounded by wilderness. My first job was to visit the post office. I was so relieved when the post office lady returned to the counter with a parcel for me. Commercial Electronics had responded quickly and flown a demonstration recorder from Scarborough, Ont., to Inuvik NWT. We celebrated in the Eskimo Hotel with Arctic Char for Heather and a delicious caribou steak for me.

June 5th was a lovely morning, so we were out on the road at about 6 am. The minidisc recorder worked perfectly and conditions for recording were good. Only occasional trucks passing or airport noises caused temporary delays in my work. The Boreal Forest reached north along the Mackenzie valley all the way to the Arctic Ocean. On each side of the road were Black Spruce, muskeg and ponds. Northern Waterthrush, Yellow-rumped Warbler, Wilson's Warbler, White-crowned Sparrow, Fox Sparrow, Lincoln's Sparrow, Savannah Sparrow, jays and raven showed up regularly as I walked along. My most pleasing recordings were of Arctic Loon. Also interesting was the presence of Wood Frogs on the edge of the Mackenzie Delta. I had never imagined that frogs could survive this far north.

After returning to town we filled up the Bird Mobile with groceries, minidiscs, materials for making moccasins and set out for one more item. On the sidewalk behind us, an old lady fell down. We were quickly there to assist her. An RCMP officer pulled up at that time, thanked us, and asked the lady her name, address and how much she had been drinking! The officer then arranged to take her home. Soon afterwards he caught up with us and leaning out of his car explained the drinking problem in Inuvik. The friendly officer wondered "if he could do anything else for us"? I couldn't ask him the question foremost in my mind, but Heather unerringly said, "Where is the liquor store?" Sadly, alcohol does not agree with the Inuit people. Inuvik has a mixture of cultures preventing a simple solution to the problem. With one main culture Fort McPherson has solved the problem by choosing to become a drug and alcohol free community. One of Inuvik's great attractions is the friendliness of all the people, typified by the RCMP officer. An Inuit lady stopped us in a store from making a purchase and advised us where to shop more economically.

Three caribou herds and a semi-domesticated reindeer herd provided a good supply of meat to the delta, but it hasn't always been so. White whalers based at Herschel Island hunted out most of the caribou in the late nineteenth century. This predation of caribou caused a change in migration routes and potential starvation for the delta Inuit. The Canadian government did several studies to determine if reindeer from Alaska could be brought in. Reindeer had been imported into Alaska from Lapland. The reindeer have shorter legs, are wider in the back and have a darker coat than the caribou. There was a herd of 3,000 animals, available under the experienced hand of a Lapland herder. The trek started in 1929 and took 6 years to complete. This is a story in itself as there was much hardship endured, but the Laplanders are a tough race of people. Some of their descendants can still be found in the Delta. This herd provides a popular source of meat in the region plus the traditional caribou herds have returned to their old migration routes. The reindeer herd has had many ups and downs with climate change and oil exploration.

The following is a cut and paste with permission from the Times Colonist, Victoria, Sunday, 2nd September, 2001, by line Ed Strusik.

"Northern Exposure-Over the years Binder, a descendant of the original Lap herders, has been watching this melodrama unfold with quiet fascination. Twice he has tried to buy the herd and it appears this third time he is going to be lucky. The deal is pretty much done. He hasn't been able to shake the curse of the reindeer: last spring Binder brought a reindeer herder from Sweden to help him move 6,000 animals from the Tuktiuktuk Peninsula to Richards Island on the Arctic coast. Everything went smoothly till the fog moved in and allowed 500 animals to break from the herd and return to the original site. Binder, however, is still confident that he has enough animals to make one of the oldest and largest reindeer ranches in North America even bigger."

The plan is to get the population up to about 12,000. "After that we'll take out about 2,000 animals each year, and send them to market down south, and hopefully to Europe." In his offer to purchase Lloyd Binder has agreed to pay the grazing fees and clear

JOHN NEVILLE

up all of the legal mess. That's why he's irked that the deal has taken almost 4 years and about $100,000 to conclude. "If I'd known 4 years ago that it would take this long, and this much paperwork, I don't think I'd have ever done it, but now it looks like she's mine." Binder seems to have no hard feelings for all of the hurdles he has had to go through. He plans to show off part of the herd this Christmas when Canadian North Airlines comes to Inuvik with Santa Claus to deliver presents to the children at the airport. "It's been a traditional thing that they do. This year we're hoping to get some reindeer in here to pull a sleigh I've got in my backyard. I figure that will spread some good will and give us a fresh start. Right now though the challenge is to find and train local people to be reindeer herders. It's a lost art in these parts", says Binder. "What few people there are who have the skills are working for the oil companies for more pay than I could ever afford, but we'll get it done even if I have to do the herding myself."

CHAPTER 11

THE RETURN JOURNEY

Including: Campbell Uplands, Sharp-tailed Grouse Lek, Aurora Borealis and Willow Ptarmigan

Just before five am June 6th, we were ready to leave Inuvik to bird along the road heading south. More motorhomes and campers had arrived yesterday - actually more than we had encountered on the whole trip. Some of them were twice as long as the Bird Mobile and the owners were spending the summer in the north. Ron, a Los Alamos based scientist was going to mass at the igloo-shaped church before heading for Anchorage and a family reunion. The GPS read N 68'21", W 133'44". The Inuvik campground is only 19 m. above the East Channel of the Mackenzie River. To my surprise we were more than 10 degrees further west than Victoria B.C.! Another curiosity is that we were still on Mountain Standard, not Pacific Time. The journey home was going to lead us down the earth's surface over 20 degrees of latitude. It was 5am and bright warm sunshine.

We travel slowly as I often walked ahead to record, or we turned off into a gravel pit or campground. The granite rocks and gravel deposits clearly pointed to the activity of the Laurentide Glacier that scraped this landscape bare just a few thousand years ago. One well-groomed trail took us across ancient bedrock with glacial scarring. It led to the Campbell Lake Lookout. The glacial process appears to have scooped out the huge basin from softer sedimentary rocks. The striations are clearly marked all around the cliffs. The Western Arctic Travel Guide told a slightly different story. The sedimentary rocks were formed as part of the ancient Mackenzie Delta and are now called the Campbell Uplift. After the downward pressure of the glacier was removed the cliffs expanded to their former height leaving a deep hollow which is now Campbell Lake. From the lookout, white ice still covered the lake. The birch and tamarack had no leafbuds like those down in the valley. Our senses were delighted by Townsend Solitaire, Bohemian Waxwings, Merlin, Yellow-rumped Warbler and my first recording of a Chipping Sparrow this trip.

In 1993 these lands were formally given back to the Gwitchen, who in turn are going to dedicate the Uplands as a park. Many cultures including our own tell stories about the origin of our planet. The Gwitchen creation myth is just as imaginative as the bible story. The Northern First Nations people tell how Crow helped to make the world habitable for animals and people. Crow carved people from a poplar tree. The archeologists think that the ancestors of the present Gwitchen have been living here for at least 8,000 years. The Inuvialuit arrived about 4,000 years ago and their ancestors tell of an older human inhabitant disappearing elsewhere when they arrived.

The increasing strength of the wind stopped my recording opportunities early that night. We camped in an old gravel pit next to a large pond. Two Arctic Loons kept us company. At 3am they began to call so I went out, in a calm environment, to record them. The sun was low in the sky but refusing to dip below the horizon. Taking a walk along the road gave me the chance to record Orange-crowned Warbler and Gray-cheeked Thrush. During the daytime both birds had moved further away from the road at my approach. This early morning both birds were singing to males in neighboring territories (counter singing) and less interested in my presence. Starting about 20 m. away to get them used to my recording profile, I gradually moved closer. On the third take I was only 5 m. away and neither bird had moved. Walking away it was very satisfying that neither bird had been disturbed and I had two close up recordings on minidisc. At 4:30 am returning to bed is a little difficult when the sparrows, thrushes and warblers are singing lustily. It is the coolest part of the day but the bed was nice and warm.

We got up late, and took a stroll onto the ridge overlooking the quarry. More rolling hills and ponds stretched into the distance. Recording equipment and camera were left behind as we enjoyed the land and the security of each other's affection. Green buds were showing and Cliff Swallows flew overhead. The dried mud retained caribou footprints. We were reluctant to leave the beautiful bird song, the blossoming of vegetation in the Mackenzie delta and the distant snowcapped Richardsons that spring morning. Falco even had a last swim before I lifted the step and closed the door. In Thinking Like A Mountain Robert Bateman said, "If we thought in the way mountains were formed we would treat the natural world with more respect" (4). His book was one of the thought-provoking tomes I reread on this part of the trip.

We stopped at the Rengleng River to look for grouse. A clearing surrounded by brush marks the most northerly known lek, aka dancing ground, for the Sharp-tailed Grouse. The males dance and call in the middle of the arena. The best performers attract the favours of most females. This lek behaviour is common to many grouse around the Northern Hemisphere from the Sage Grouse of the Great Plains to the Black Grouse of the Scottish Highlands. The performances take place in spring, but we were too late, and there were no grouse near the lek. We had seen two birds earlier in an old quarry a few km. further north. This is a large grouse about 43cm. tall, with a speckled chest and a dark back. The under part of the wedge-shaped tail is white.

On June 8th I stood across the road from a busy creek and recorded the soft plaintive calls of a beaver. I believe it was a begging call of the kit, although I'm not absolutely sure. When I stepped across the road the adult beaver could see me for the first time. It raised the alarm with a loud "splosh" of its tail and kept circling in the middle of the creek to maintain my attention. The alarm signal would also keep the kits hidden. Heather came up and scanned the banks with her binoculars but could not locate the youngsters.

About 20 km. north of Tsiigehtchic (Arctic Red River) and the ferry crossing I had another memorable walk. At 3, 4 and 5 in the morning, the avian soundscape was all about me. The trees were clothed with new leaves and the ice had disappeared from the ponds. The richest and often the loudest songsters were the Fox Sparrow, Northern Waterthrush and White-crowned Sparrow. Other birds making regular appearances were Lincoln's Sparrow, Yellow Warbler, Gray-cheeked and Swainson's Thrush, Wilson's Snipe and Wilson's Warbler. As we passed ponds there was usually a male Arctic Loon in residence and twice long wailing calls were given. The sweet trills of Spotted Sandpiper were also audible. Quieter songs of Hermit Thrush, Cliff and Bank's Swallow overhead and the insect-like sounds of the Blackpoll Warbler could be heard. The curious little ticking sound of the blackpolls along the side of the road carries well due to the low frequency element of their song. Occasionally, a Hawk Owl crossed my path with its thrilling warble and the distant bugling of Sandhill Crane echoed. Only 4 days earlier, as we travelled north, the leaves were still in bud; there was still ice evident on the ponds; Swainson's Thrush

TRAVELLING THE DEMPSTER

and Spotted Sandpiper, amongst others, had not started to sing. This was perhaps the peak moment of spring in the Delta. We had witnessed the change of the season in just a few short days.

As we waited for the ferry another traveller told us of his enjoyable flight to Tuk (Tuktoyaktuk). He said there was a crazy maze of islands in the Delta and at Tuk you could look out onto the ice of the Arctic ocean, seeing local people using skidoos to travel far from the shore. They also flew over one of the largest pingos in Canada. Pingos are upthrusts in the permafrost and usually circular. The one he referred to was about 50 meters tall. The ferry only stopped long enough to load the five waiting vehicles and was off. He reversed out and allowed the current to take us downstream. When he changed into forward gear, there was sudden silence causing us to miss a heartbeat! Perhaps we were going to see Tuk after all! Fortunately, the engine soon kicked in and we headed upstream to our landing.

The confluence of these two rivers is still a meeting place for the Gwitchen people and fishing remains an important activity. Our destination for the evening was again Frog Creek. On our visit going north, Heather went to the fish camp. A local elder was smoking freshly caught White fish by hanging them over the beams of a small log smokehouse. Heather purchased two nice fish for ten dollars. Tonight two more fish steaks were to be baked and garnished with egg, bread crumbs, basil, and pepper, and served with broccoli, noodles and mushroom soup. The fish is a sweet delicate flavour but you have to watch for bones.

The following morning, I stopped below a Northern Hawk Owl who was consuming a small mammal. After he had finished breakfast, he vocalised into my microphone for several minutes. There were no warbles, but hard whistled notes, which may be alarm calls. It was a good closeup recording with only distant birds in

JOHN NEVILLE

the background.

When we reached the Peel crossing, the ferry landings were still being worked on. The river was now about 5 meters below the original flood line and still falling. As the river slowly receded the landing had to be extended outwards with dry gravel. However, we were able to drive on and off without difficulty.

As we ascended the Richardsons, these rugged mountains enveloped us. We stopped and felt the heaviness upon us that some people call "the silence of the north." The gray surfaces around us had changed to green in a few days. Slumping areas punctuated the landscape, where thawing permafrost had allowed the top soil to slip and sag downwards with gravity. As we ascended higher into the canyon country the greens of grass and leaves were intruding amongst the grays of cliff and shale. A large mass of purple bloom attracted Heather's camera. The flowers were emerging from a rocky crevice. Perhaps the most spectacular image for us was a Golden Eagle gliding silently into a rock perch just above, and ahead of the Bird Mobile. His wings were just about as wide as our vehicle. Eagles are usually very nervous of man (understandably so). Therefore, we were surprised to have such a close up encounter. It took us more than an hour to drive from the Peel lowlands to the summit of the Richardsons, representing the depth of the old Laurentide glacier! No wonder the rocks around Campbell Lake were compressed.

Travelling in the north makes one so much more aware, not only of the seasons, but the factors in the universe which cause them. The main reason is the 23 degree tilt of the earth and its annual orbit around the sun. On June 11th the Northern Hemisphere is only 10 days from its closest position to the sun. Daylight is almost continuous, hence the midnight sun.

Travelling the Dempster

In the winter darkness, another earthly phenomenon occurs, called the Northern Lights. In our hemisphere, the technical name is Aurora Borealis and in the south, Aurora Austrailis. For countless generations humans thought the light was emitted from another world. They were more or less correct. During the space age much of the mystery of these beautiful lights has been unravelled. Rocket borne equipment has detected charged particles, known as plasma, emitted from the sun. This thin stream of plasma is carried towards the earth on the cosmic wind. It sweeps around the planet zeroing in on the magnetic fields at the poles. When the particles cross the magnetic field tremendous amounts of electricity are generated. Negative electrons are then drawn towards the Earth following the lines of the magnetic fields. The electrons tumble and swirl in broad curtains like eddies in water. As they enter the upper atmosphere they briefly energize other particles. The particles in oxygen produce green light and those in nitrogen create pink light. This is the light we know as the Aurora Borealis.

The fantastic roping movements, dancing in perfect harmony of sky and earth. (6) The colours moved through the trees with a sound so hushed it was like softly moving silk. (22)

Sometimes they shoot rathlike across the sky like smoke in a wind tunnel. (7) This is a spectacle usually limited to the winter months. However, travelling north on Haida Gwaii towards Massett in June, 1999, we witnessed the Aurora with just white light dancing down the sky.

When we arrived at the Arctic Circle pullout, I was reminded more about the northern extremity of the planet. This imaginary line at North 66 degrees , 33 minutes is the circle around which the sun does not set on June 21st. The further north you go from this point the more days of total light occur on either side of the summer soltice. The reverse occurs on December 21st when it is

JOHN NEVILLE

dark for the full 24 hours. In reality, there is some reflected light allowing people to work outdoors around midday.

Reaching the Eagle Plains Hotel we noticed some changes: the summer staff had arrived and there were a number of tourists in the dining room. The new staff seemed just as friendly as the ones we knew. An example of making do on the Dempster occurred just after we arrived. A small plane landed on the road, taxied back to the hotel, crossed the carpark and stopped at the fuel pump. After taking on gas, he turned around and used the road to takeoff.

Crossing Eagle Plains, we stopped for a Black Bear climbing a cliff. He was taking a zig-zag course and then disappeared into a chimney to make the rest of the ascent. About 30 minutes later across the plain a buff-coloured momma grizzly appeared near the road. She stood to her full 2.2 m., as others of her kind had done, to scent the Bird Mobile. She quickly turned and led her two small black cubs away through the spruce trees. The bear count increased to 8 Grizzly and 7 Black Bear.

As we proceded south along the Ogilvie River, its waters had subsided 3 to 5 m. The section of road previously threatened now had warning signs for a "washout." One half of the road was still in good shape. My luck was in as we approached Windy Pass. There was no wind and the Gyrfalcon allowed me to record her plaintive calls for a few minutes. The sound was similar to a Prairie Falcon. There are only 750 pairs of these magnificent falcons in all of the Yukon. Ptarmigan are their main food source. We later heard from Dave Mossop, a noted biologist in the area, that the pair had failed to raise this year's chicks. The cause was unknown.

An added bonus were the Western Wood Pewees on the opposite cliff. Their two part whistled notes carried quite well down to the microphone. This is beyond the recorded northern limit for this member of the flycatcher family (1). The lovely sounds of a

TRAVELLING THE DEMPSTER

Townsend Solitaire, a member of the thrush family, enthralled us a little further down the pass. The sound was all the more enjoyable amongst the harsh rocky scenery.

Chapman , in the Blackstone valley, is the largest lake along the Dempster and had several pairs of Red-throated Loons. Their calls have an eerie quality. The Blackstone Uplands are an attractive birding area with many lakes. Henry David Thoreau said: "A lake is the landscape's most beautiful and expressive feature. It is the earth's eye, looking into which, the beholder measures the depth of his own nature." (16)

One evening we had a pleasant surprise. Two cyclists pulled into our campsite: Dirk and Angi (pronouned Anya)whom we had last spoken to near Arctic Red River, 400 km. up the road. They were peddling from Inuvik to Argentina, and taking at least three years to fulfill their dream of seeing the Americas. Dirk said they had sold all of their belongings in Belgium in order to make the trip. What they really enjoyed were the friendly people along the Dempster. The next day we passed one group of birders out on the tundra near a microwave tower and a second party near the outfitters camp before pulling into the Tombstone Campground.

Tombstone Mountains photo by Cameron Eckert

It was June 12th, a Saturday night, and Yukon birders filled the campground. We were able to return some books to Julie

JOHN NEVILLE

Frisch who had kindly allowed us to take them on the road. In the evening, all the birders got together in the cookhouse to drink tea and listen to Dave Mossop. He gave a fascinating talk about the life of ptarmigan along the highway.

The male Willow Ptarmigan are highly territorial in the spring. Their spring plumage makes them very noticeable to fox, Gyrfalcon and Golden Eagle. This allows the female to go unnoticed as she incubates her eggs. In the winter they are quite gregarious, living in large flocks, sometimes including Rock and White-tailed Ptarmigan. If they are attacked by fox or Gyrfalcon, most have a chance to escape. During the winter they stay hidden in the snow except emerging to browse twice a day. The birds can eat about half their body weight in small willow twigs in a single day and then slowly digest the food. Amazingly, they are able to continue putting on weight throughout the winter! Dave handed round a ptarmigan foot, the remains of something else's dinner. He wanted us to see the delicate appendages which grow out of the claws just like long finger nails. Their function is to further spread the weight load when walking on soft snow. The feathers around the feet also have this function. In spring time, walking on rocks and gravel quickly wears away the appendages. The ptarmigan beak is also adapted for winter feeding. Like the voles, lemming, hare, moose and caribou these ptarmigan convert the seemingly limited vegetation into meat which predator birds and mammals, like ourselves, consume further up the foodchain.

Driving down the highway the following morning we slowed for a cluster of birders gathered near a creek. They had a spotting scope focused into a Spruce tree. We stopped and were able to confirm their suspicion that they were looking at and listening to their first Gray-cheeked Thrush! The Dempster had yielded another bounty to a very appreciative audience.

POSTSCRIPT

After returning home with many happy memories of our adventures, I got to work on my next CD called "Bird Songs of the Arctic". My target was 90 species on a 2 CD set. I had enough good recordings for about 75 of the animals to be featured. The script was another part of the project which needed work and refinement.

In addition to carefully documenting my recordings along the Dempster I wrote a basic text for the narration which divided the Dempster into its different regions. After some thought I added a section called "Beyond the Dempster" to cover some of the species in the Mackenzie Delta and the High Arctic. Some people will want to hear those critters before undertaking a major travel itinerary. By the end of August my script was in good enough shape to start reading it out loud. I usually chose times when no one else could hear me until I was sure of the content. The wording gradually changed to fit my speaking voice right up to the week when I entered a studio in November. During the last few weeks I read confidently with no worries if Heather was within earshot. The challenge is to pack as much information as possible into two or three sentences. I want to be informative without dominating the birds who are the real stars. A critic once said, "It's like sitting on a log in the middle of the woods with John. The birds are all around and he tells you about them quietly while listening to the bird song". The key is to be unobtrusive and yet share the identification and some knowledge about the avian subject.

I was lacking good recordings (or none at all) for about 15 species. My final target was 90 birds and other animals. To obtain the remaining species I approached other nature recordists who had recorded in the area. Their participation was greatly appreciated and a list of their names will appear in the CD acknowledgements. One example was Ted Miller. I learned he had recorded a Surfbird in the late 1970's in the company of Bob and Julie Frisch. Ted's last known address was in Victoria, I eventually tracked him down in St. John's Newfoundland!

In late November I finally entered a studio. Traz Damji's studio is situated on the 22nd storey of a downtown highrise in Vancouver. The space is filled with state of the art equipment. My new sound engineer is very easy to get along with, like his predecessor. Even so, my throat becomes sore quickly when speaking into a microphone. I had managed to create the same state of tension a few days earlier at home when rehearsing. It's hard to explain the sore throat which has only happened while recording the last 2 CD's. Warm water helps and some rehearsal without speaking out-loud conserved my voice. About 10 hours of work had all the script completed. But our first day was not finished: we continued with the bird recordings for another 2 hours. It had been a good day. The following morning, Saturday, we continued to work through my pile of recordings for another 12 hours. The whole process took 24 hours out of 2 days. Expressing my thoughts to an imaginary audience was challenging and ultimately quite satisfying. Small glitches like me tapping the microphone can be electronically removed by the engineer. The result turns a good recording into a very good recording. Unfortunately, recordings with constant noise, such as a plane or a loud river, can only be improved partially without spoiling the subject matter. Overall the studio experience is satisfying as it draws on my artistic and technical abilities. Perhaps like someone who creates a painting.

When I first came to Canada in 1975 there were very few recordings available from which I could learn North American bird songs. As my curiosity and sometimes frustration grew, I became interested in nature recording. A workshop from Cornell University in 1993 gave me the confidence to get started. In 1994, I produced enough recordings to enter the Cornell Laboratory of Ornithology studio and create "Birds of the Kootenays". I did not rehearse myself enough and the process took five days. Plus I barely had enough good recordings for the project. The following year I also took five days at the CBC studio in Toronto creating "Bird Songs of the Creston Valley". The last 2 CD's have each taken a total of 2 long days. The time in a studio is fulfilling but still a challenge. My production events occur about once every two years so I am not fully at ease with the process. Perhaps that is why my voice has been resisting the stresses. However, the pleasure gained is sometimes enormous! It is very gratifying when a bank clerk I barely know runs up and throws her arms around me saying, "From your CD I finally know the name of a bird I heard in my childhood." Those are very precious moments for a Nature Recordist.

On the 9th of February I received a copy of the first 10 tracks from Traz. It was a pleasure to listen to the narration and bird subjects starting to come together as one entity. However, the Sharp-shinned Hawk was too short and several other comments needed to be made. The sound engineer wants to know exactly what I want, so it's very important for me to listen very carefully, then respond. For example, the red squirrel started with one call of a warbler, then the squirrel appeared with a robin. The robin's song was just as loud as the squirrel. On the original recording that was how it started. Halfway through the robin takes a break and there is a lovely closeup of the squirrel alone. I asked Traz to use the second half of the recording and cut out the first warbler song. Many of the people listening are using the recording to help with their own animal identification, therefore leaving in the warbler's one song is confusing. Also the robin was not only too loud but caused confusion to the listener and made the squirrel more difficult to focus on. On the plus side, Traz had been twin tracking the recordings which produces a virtual stereo effect. I was delighted to hear the added depth that twin tracking creates. I am not quite sure how the technology works but the background atmosphere is definitely enhanced. The end result is a more realistic environment on the recording.

Friday, March 4th, was another memorable day! The first full copy of the 2 CD set arrived. There are still some corrections to be made but the overall soundscape was better than I had hoped. After Traz has made a few more minor changes the recording will go to Music Manufacturers in Toronto where the master copy will be turned into a first edition of "Bird Songs of the Arctic". As this last stage evolves Heather takes over responsibility for the artwork. A suitable picture has to be chosen for the front cover and the print material has to be prepared for the insert tray. The details are finalized on the internet subject to Heather's approval and then manufacturing can begin. The 2 CD set should be released in July, 2005. I began researching the project in the fall of 2003. As I write, the preliminary work is almost completed for the next recording, "Bird Songs of the Scottish Highlands and Islands". The field trip begins on May 1st and a similar pattern will emerge through to completion in the summer of 2006.

OTHER RECORDINGS
BY JOHN NEVILLE

Birds of the Kootenays CD , 1994
Bird Songs of the Creston Valley CD, 1995
Bird Songs of the Okanagan CD, 1996
Songs and Sounds of the Canadian Rockies CD, 1997
Bird Songs of Canada's West Coast CD, 1999
Bird Songs of the Great Lakes CD, 2002
Beginners Guide to B.C. Bird Song 2CD set by
Mel Coulson and John Neville, 2003
Bird Songs-Western Boreal Forest 2CD set, 2004
Bird Songs of the Arctic 2CD set, 2005

All these recordings are still available and can be found at
web site www.nevillerecording.com

THE BIBLIOGRAPHY

1. Alexander, Stuart A. et al. Birds of the Yukon Territory. Vancouver: UBC Press, 2003.

2. Aspin, Jean. Arctic Daughter. Minneapolis, MN: Bergamost Books, 1988.

3. Backhouse, Francis. Women of the Klondike. Vancouver: Whitecap Books, 1996.

4. Bateman, Robert. Thinking Like a Mountain. Toronto: Viking, 2000.

5. Bonnycastle, R.H.G. (Richard Henry Gardyne), 1903-1968. ed. Heather Robertson. A Gentleman Adventurer: The Arctic Diaries of R.H.G. Bonnycastle. Toronto: Lester & Orpen Dennys, 1984.

6. Brennan, Anne T. The Real Klondike Kate. Fredericton, NB: Goose Lane, 1990.

7. Bryson, Bill. Neither Here Nor There: Travels in Europe. New York: Morrow, 1992.

8. Burger, Joanna. The Parrot Who Owns Me. New York: Villard Books, 2001.

9. Burton, Laura Beatrice. I Married The Klondike: McClelland and Stewart, Toronto, 1954&1961 .

10. Burton, Pierre. Klondike. The Last Great Goldrush. Toronto: McClelland and Stewart, 1972.

11. Burton, Pierre. Drifting Home. Toronto: McClelland and Stewart, 1973.

12. Calef, George W. (George Waller). Journey: The Dempster Highway: A Travellers' Guide to the Land and Its People. Whitehorse: Yukon Conservation Society, 1984.

13. Coates, Kenneth S. "The Lost Patrol". Horizon Canada, English E edition(Jan 2001),pn.pagop2maps3c7bw.

JOHN NEVILLE

14. Corley-Smith, Peter. 10,000 Hours: A Helicopter Pilot in the North. Victoria, BC: Sono Nis Press, 1995.
15. Day, David. Noah's Choice. London: Penguin, 1990.
16. Erickson, George. True North: Exploring the Great Canadian Wilderness by Bush Plane. Toronto: Thomas Allen, 2000.
17. Fiennes, William. The Snow Geese: A Story of Home. Toronto: Random House Canada, 2002.
18. Frisch, Robert. Birds by the Dempster Highway. Edition 2nd rev. Morriss Printing. 1987.
19. Gough, Barry M. Gold Rush! Toronto: Grolier, 1983.
20. Graef, Kris V. The Milepost. Edition 56th. Augusta: Morris Communication, 2004.
21. Harley, Jack. "The Mad Trapper of Rat River" NWT 26 Sept, 2004. <www.mysteriesofcanada/NWT/madtrapper.htm>
22. Hatfield, Fred. North of the Sun: A Memoir of the Alaskan Wilderness. New York: Birch Lane, 1990.
23. Hill, Bill. "Dempster Highway." History Notes, 26 Sept, 2004. <http://www3.sympatico.ca/billh56/>
24. Krause, Bernard L. Wild Soundscapes: Discovering the Voice of the Natural World: a book and cd recording. 1st ed. Berkley: Wilderness Press, 2002.
25. Lanz, Walter. Along the Dempster: An Outdoor Guide to Canada's Northern Most Highway. 1st ed. Vancouver: Oak House Publishing, 1985. 2nd ed. 1990. 3rd ed. 2002.
26. MacKenzie, Sir Alexander. First Man West: Alexander Mackenzie's journal of his voyage to the Pacific coast of Canada in 1793 / edited by Walter Sheppe PUBLISHER: Westport, Conn. : Greenwood Press, 1976, c1962. NOTES: First ed. published in 1801 under title: Voyages from Montreal. Includes index. Reprint of the ed. published by the University of California Press, Berkley. Bibliography: p. 353-

357.

27. May, Denny. "WopMay.com." 26 Sept, 2004. <http://www.
wopmay.com/wm.asp?lid=1>

28. Minter, Roy. The White Pass: Gateway to the Klondike.
Toronto: McClelland and Stewart, 1987.

29. Mowat, Farley. People of the Deer. Toronto: McClelland &
Stewart, 1975.

30. Neville, John. Bird Songs-Western Boreal Forest: CD, Neville
Recording, 2004.

31. Newman, Peter C. Company of Adventurers. Markham, Ont.:
Viking, 1985.

32. North, Dick.The Mad Trapper of Rat River.Toronto:
Macmillan,1976.

33. North, Dick. Trackdown. Toronto: Macmillan, 1989.

34. Pynn, Larry. The Forgotten Trail: One Man's Adventures on
the Canadian Route to the Klondike. Toronto: Doubleday
Canada Ltd., 1996.

35. Savours, Ann. The Search for the North West Passage. New
York: St. Martin's Press, 1999.

36. Saunders, Gary. Alder Music. St. John's, NFLD: Breakwater,
1989.

37. Stefansson, Vilhjalmur. The Friendly Arctic, the Story of
Five Years in Polar Regions. New York :The Macmillan
Company, 1921.

38. Stewart, Robert. Sam Steele: Lion of the Frontier. Toronto:
Doubleday, 1979.

39. Suzuki, David. The Ghost Walker: The Nature of Things.
CBC TV, Vancouver, March 17, 2004.

40. Taylor, Leonard W. The Sourdough and the Queen: The
Many Lives of Klondike Joe Boyle. Toronto: Methuen, 1983.

JOHN NEVILLE

41. Weiner, Jonathan. The Beak of the Finch: A Story of
    Evolution in Our Time. New York: Knopf, 1994.
42. Wilson, Ian and Sally. Gold Rush: Reliving the Klondike
    Adventure in Canada's North. West Vancouver, BC: Gordon
    Soules Book Publishers Ltd., 1996.
43. Young, Steven B. To the Arctic: An Introduction to the Far
    Northern World. New York : Wiley, c1988, c1989, c1994.

ISBN 1-41205830-9